THE LITTLE BOOK
OF OUTDOOR WISDOM

An Adventurer's Collection of Anecdotes and Advice

JOHN LONG

FALCON

GUILFORD, CONNECTICUT

FALCON®

An imprint of The Rowman & Littlefield Publishing Group, Inc.
4501 Forbes Blvd., Ste. 200
Lanham, MD 20706
www.rowman.com

Falcon and FalconGuides are registered trademarks and Make Adventure Your Story is a
trademark of The Rowman & Littlefield Publishing Group, Inc.

Distributed by NATIONAL BOOK NETWORK

British Library Cataloguing in Publication Information available

Library of Congress Cataloging-in-Publication Data available

ISBN 978-1-4930-3473-4 (hardcover)
ISBN 978-1-4930-3474-1 (e-book)

♾™ The paper used in this publication meets the minimum requirements of American
National Standard for Information Sciences—Permanence of Paper for Printed Library
Materials, ANSI/NISO Z39.48-1992.

Contents

Contents

Introduction

An editor I work with mentioned that sales for Edward Abbey's *Desert Solitaire* have remained steady for fifty years. His marketing department deconstructed the text every which way but could never determine what made the book so evergreen, except perhaps Abbey's knack for angering both liberals and rednecks at the same time.

I loved Abbey, wilderness bard and best-selling author of *The Money Wrench Gang*, which in 1975 thundered through the literary world like chain lightning. Abbey was at his cranky best when he'd rant about "sons and daughters of The Pioneers." That's us. We'd gone soft, said Abbey, had lost our sense of the primitive and remote, our hunger for the difficult, the original, the real, none more than Abbey's fellow rangers (circa 1965) at Arches National Park.

"Make the bums range," wrote Abbey. "Yank them out of air conditioned offices and shiny patrol cars and dump them at the trail head, where they belong, tromping in and out of the wilderness, hiking off that office fat and getting their minds off the other guy's wife.

"Let them get lost, sunburned, stranded, drowned, eaten by bears, buried under avalanches . . . the right and privilege of any free American."

He warned about our mania for information, predicted the day, now upon us, where virtual reality could threaten to replace direct experience. We needed to renew old skills: to follow a trail over slickrock, build a fire in the rain, treat snakebite, glissade down a glacier, bury a body, cook a porcupine, or "pour piss out of a boot."

This fiery talk plays to the cowboy in many of us, but how many of the young among us would consider getting attacked by bears or buried by avalanche a right and privilege? Probably fewer would equate these things with freedom, as Abbey did. It gets wild out there. You can't control the rain and rattlesnakes. It costs time and money—sometimes a lot of it—to get there. Isn't it better to stay closer to home, forget the slickrock, and let Edward bury the body?

Abbey's all-or-nothing approach is uncompromising, and that's the power of the purist. But there are options between a country path winding through Sonoma wine country and the North Face of K2, one of the hardest big mountains in the world.

As renowned alpinist Herman Buhl once said, "Tastes differ." So do temperaments and physical capacities. Few people profit from full immersion into the wilderness. It might be good medicine for rangers in national parks, with their training and instruction. Most of the rest of us—and the path followed in this book—will favor a softer approach. A fling with The Remote is better than nothing, but a romance, one that can sustain us, usually takes time.

Nature shows us a nearly infinite patience for things to emerge and develop. It also takes from a little to a lot of equipment, depending on our activity and the given terrain, and a vast array of techniques and practical know-how (read: *experience*).

Thing is, outdoor gear is always evolving. The federal Bureau of Economic Analysis (BEA) says the current outdoor recreation industry comprises 2 percent ($373.7 billion) of the entire US Gross Domestic Product, making it a bigger industry than oil and mining. The competition to get a piece of that pie is fierce, ergo the fantastic array of available gear, much of it unnecessary. Even the wilderness itself, owing to global warming, logging, strip-mining, and so forth, is changing, mostly for the worse. The point is, staying current with equipment, techniques, and topography is an ongoing study; and while we touch on these topics, as needed, the thrust of this book is not about gear, techniques, or geography. A million blogs and websites can keep you current in that, but they can mislead.

A common outdoor myth is that so long as your gear and skill are up to speed, and you understand the given activity and terrain, you're basically good to go. Any experienced outdoors person will tell you this is a mistake. The World Cup skier will want her "boards" tuned just so before vaulting down the Hahnenkamm downhill course in the Kitzbühel Alps of Austria, one of the greatest spectacles in outdoor adventure sports; but winning the Hahnenkamm, or even laying down a successful run, always involves more than state-of-the-art skis, honed skill, and courage. It requires developing an approach that puts a person in the best position to thrive. Not in some abstract way, rather one derived from factors and forces as basic as sand. Such an approach is never an equation. It's never simply facts and figures, or bullet points in a web page. It is not easily explained, but the process can be described.

The last few lines in Norman Maclean's classic, *A River Runs Through It*, reads, "Eventually, all things merge into one, and a river runs through it. The river was cut by the world's great flood and runs over rocks from the basement of time. On some of the rocks are timeless raindrops. Under the rocks are the words, and some of the words are theirs."

—◠—

My hope for this small volume is that "their" words are echoed throughout these pages—words said to me directly, words I overheard, words I conjured from many years of rubbing elbows, and in some cases sharing a rope, with people for whom the outdoors ran though their veins like a river in flood. Words that take up where gear and skill leave off, and demonstrate an approach to *being and acting* in the wild places that has stood the test of time.

Preparation

AVOIDING TROUBLE

When heading into the wilds to explore a cave, or just following a dusty trail up a popular peak, how do we appraise and manage potential risks? The intuitive method is a poor choice, but it makes for rich stories. One of my favorites comes from Dave Diegleman, when he, Dale Bard, and the great, late Jim Bridwell were gearing up to climb a big new route in Yosemite Valley.

"The morning we set sail on the *Sea of Dreams* route," said Dave, "we got to our fixed ropes at the base of El Capitan and each of us fished around for our harnesses, which we'd stashed under rocks the day before. Dale and I quickly found ours and strapped them on, but Jim was farting around in the forest below.

'Um, we're sorta ready to go,' I mumbled, loud enough for the old guy to hear.

'I gotta find a stick,' Jim snapped. Moments later, unable to see beneath the boulder, he fishes out his harness, and a baby rattlesnake slithers out right after."

Bridwell had this sixth sense, or guardian angels, or intuitive voodoo that saw him through some of the wildest outdoor adventures in modern times. The rest of us will want a more objective method to appraise and manage risks.

Our experience outdoors occurs along two spectrums: *presence to performance* and *length of stay*. Most of the material in this book is described in those terms.

The person who pulls over their car and walks to the scenic overlook is merely present, observing. Should they hike around the pond, they are starting to *do* something in the outdoors. If they tromp up that mountain, and later learn rope management and safety skills, they've entered adventure sports, and the world of performance, which runs, for instance, from simple ski touring, to surfing 50-foot waves at Jaws, in Maui.

On the time spectrum, the casual hiker might take two hours hiking the out-and-back up the local fire road. The arctic explorer could spend two months on the ice pack, physically cut off from civilization.

While *what* we do outdoors runs the gamut, and our length of stays vary, sometimes greatly, trip to trip, *our basic strategy for staying safe remains the same.*

The basic strategy is, *never push danger and difficulty at the same time.* This metric is simple in principle. What makes it tricky is that risk is mitigated by skill, which makes *difficulty* a relative term. Consider mountain biking. If riding off the trail lands you on a gently angled grass slope, the danger is probably minimal. If the edge of the trail drops off a cliff, the *potential danger* is high. The *real danger,* however, is determined by the *difficulty* of a given rider to stay on the trail.

Even with a cliff drop, an intermediate rider should have little *difficulty* safely riding a flat, 10-foot-wide fire road. If the going feels scary, you get off and walk. But what if the trail is a steep, rocky singletrack, snaking down crumbly terrain? The pro rider might succeed, but the intermediate biker could easily take the big drop. Throw in some obstacles and big air, and the pro is looking at a hard landing as well. The consequences are constant; the difficulty is relative.

Good judgment requires knowing where your limits lie, and when there's doubt, backing off. You can't improve without pushing your limits (*difficulty*), but do so where the consequences (*danger*) are limited, not on a singletrack with a cliff drop. If the consequences are bone crushing, make sure the course is easy *for you.*

If you challenge the danger and difficulty at the same time, you're not asking for trouble. You're making it.

TICKLING DRAGONS

"When you're out there and you're tickling the dragon," wrote Christian Beckwith, founder of *Alpinist* magazine, "you have an appreciation for the fragility of life. And you don't get that without having the dragon wake up sometimes."

The dragon, in Beckwith's case, was an avalanche that swept him and a fellow skier 1,000 vertical feet down a snow couloir (narrow chute) in the Grand Tetons, killing his partner (one of roughly thirty people killed in avalanches every year in the American backcountry, which attracts better than four million travelers a year).

An avalanche is one of the cruelest dragons found in the wilderness, and often go unseen—till they wake suddenly, hangry as hell.

I've seen downpours turn pedestrian trails in the Hollywood hills into frightening mudslides in the time it takes to pull on a raincoat. During the Pipeline Masters surf competition on the North Shore of Oahu, I heard of a wave breaking, flowing up onto the beach and washing a spectator out, nearly drowning her before lifeguards dove in and fished her out, hacking up half the Pacific. Accidents happen in a flash.

The dragon sleeps, often deeply, but it never dies. Heat, cold, gravity, currents, wind shears, and other factors all draw one conclusion: *Outdoor education is an essential part of the outdoors life.* Anyone venturing around big mountains, for instance, must understand snow science. We need to know where dragons lie, and how to live around them. That's part of being prepared.

The point was driven home for me years after I wrote a collection of books on technical adventure sports, and how people kept coming up to me saying if it hadn't been for one or another of those books, they might have died. That was the best compensation for all those dog days writing manuals "dry as a hobo's elbow." Technical writing is *work*. But everyone gets something practical from the good stuff.

⟨───⟩

There are comprehensive courses covering every square foot of The Remote, which are interesting studies in their own right, above and beyond their usefulness to the specialist. There's no chance I'll ever strap on tanks and go cave diving, but I went to a series of lectures on the subject for the sheer pleasure of knowing I'd never have to use that knowledge.

Thirst!

On my first big rock climb we made good time and got most of the way up the "East Face" of Washington Column, in Yosemite Valley, before we bivouacked on "Overnight Ledge," 300 feet from the top. We wolfed down some salami and cheese and finished the last of our water. No worries. We could get through the night OK and climb off the wall in a few hours the next morning. We'd tank up on water once we got down.

We slouched back, shoulder to shoulder on the little granite bench, blue stars winking back at us. It felt like being in church—till a hankering for a sip of water morphed into brain-frying, soul-murdering thirst. We'd climbed all day and maybe drank a quart per man—roughly eight quarts shy of the required dose. All night long we stared at the moon, trying to will it across the sky.

We summited in a daze, our mouths and eyes glued shut. I hardly recall trundling down North Dome Gully, or reeling through the Ahwahnee Hotel, across the golf course as tourists in Polo shirts watched three zombies bushwhack through the forest toward Mirror Lake, where we dove in fully clothed.

Kant said that we never experience *the thing-in-itself*, rather we experience a phenomenon as it appears to us observers. If I could pull Kant from the grave and stick him on Overnight Ledge for a few days in the burning sun, the old fart would cry "scheisse!" as he directly experienced *thirst-in-itself.*

HYDRATION: IT'S EVERYTHING!

I know a girl in Switzerland, whose neighbor is Scottish and is married to a Welshman, who knew a woman in London, who wrote a book about her father, Raymond Green, the English doctor who discovered that hydration was key to climbing big mountains. Green was on-site for the first ascent of Mount Everest, in 1953, and had convinced a doubting Edmund Hillary that if he and partner Tenzing Norgay stayed properly hydrated, their chance of summiting Everest was excellent. If they got dehydrated, as happened during every other attempt on the peak, defeat was a certainty.

Green was right, and Everest was finally climbed (the Swiss, the previous year, would surely have succeeded if they understood about hydration), but the findings of Dr. Green, a notoriously thorny character, were downplayed. It took the public another thirty years to fully appreciate the direct correlation between hydration and performance. For the modern-day outdoors person, once we understand the crucial need to stay hydrated, the means are a three-step dance.

A: Keep Drinking

Drink plenty of water, and keep drinking throughout the day. People can know this and still get dehydrated because they underestimate the amount of fluid needed for strenuous work in both hot and cold weather. Dry mountain air, along with the moisture lost through breathing (you're sucking down each breath at higher altitudes), can mummify a person climbing a mountain of ice in a rainstorm. Heat, humidity, exertion, and clothing also affect our hydration needs.

It's not just physical performance that is compromised by dehydration. Our judgment and wherewithal declines, sometimes alarmingly so, and in ways we're unaware of since our minds are dulled from lack of water. Statistics suggest that many accidents (the majority are the result of human error, and are avoidable) occur when people are tired and dehydrated—perhaps the best of all reasons to stay ahead of thirst.

B: How Much?

The *amount* of water we need to stay hydrated depends on many factors, and no one can say how much and how often a given person should drink across all conditions, but some general norms are worth reviewing.

Per amounts, the Army Manual on Desert Operations says that vigorous activity in direct sunlight requires at least two quarts of water per man per hour, or four gallons a day per man. Granted, few of us will find ourselves marching a full load across the Gobi Desert at high noon, and humping four gallons of water (33.3 pounds!) on a hike or climb is totally impractical. But the Army Manual does tell us the magnitude of the challenge. Believe it: This is not an exaggeration. A former Israeli commando told me that when his unit was conducting drills around the Dead Sea, they drank an astonishing eight gallons of water a day, per man. The only way to do so is to *stay ahead of thirst and drink all the time*, which makes sense because we're sweating the whole time, though it evaporates if we're on a bike, or often goes unnoticed in water sports. Till we bonk.

Very few conditions require constant guzzling. Casual sipping at frequent intervals is a no-lose strategy. Some advise that thirst is our best indicator of how much we need to drink, and that drinking to thirst is the simplest way to stay hydrated. Maybe so if you're bird watching or hiking on a trail, but for adventure sports athletes fully immersed in a task this is poor advice because difficult, high-effort work requires our full attention, especially when risk is involved. When so engaged we often forget to drink till we're *dying* of thirst.

Rule of thumb: If you wait till you're thirsty, you've waited too long. Keep drinking at regular intervals. Even the most demanding adventure sports are usually done in spurts, with a little downtime between burns, runs, or tries. Make it a habit to always drink a little when you're not engaged. A hands-free hydration system is helpful here—if using one is possible.

Again, *always stay ahead of thirst*, if only by a sip or two.

C: Hydration Aids

Hundreds of hydration aids (powders, liquids, and gels) are available. Electrolyte replacements are especially helpful. Cheaper "sports drinks" are often too freighted with salt and sugars for the massive liquid consumption required during peak exertion, though diluting down the mix is a common strategy, and will work to a degree.

The better sports drinks often contain some measure of protein and carbs along with electrolytes. It is important to keep the body's carbohydrate content up when exercising, and mixing in protein is helpful in this regard, as the body can metabolize these mixtures faster than food. Still, many professional athletes snack little or not at all during competitions, going instead with straight water, or using hydration aids sparingly, for a little boost. Just so you know, the ubiquitous Gatorade™ coolers seen on the sidelines of many professional sports teams are mostly full of water.

In short: Keep drinking fluids before, during, and after every outing. Learn how much you need for given trips and excursions, and take a little more. Use a hydration system whenever possible, and experiment with hydration aids to discover what works for you. Remember the Cardinal Rule: *Always stay ahead of thirst.*

GRUB

Tim ran ocean kayak tours out of Santa Monica, California, and was always searching for qualified guides. I wasn't qualified, certified, or even housebroken, but I was living in a kayak back then and sometimes would fill in when one of Tim's regular guides was hungover or went missing for whatever reason. The tours started early every weekend and were over by noon. Any later and the wind picked up, the ocean started swirling, and clients either freaked out or flopped over; and it was epic getting their boats emptied out in open water, wheedling them back into the cockpit, and leading them back to shore.

Most clients were content to paddle out a few miles and bob around and go swimming in what felt like dangerous waters. Sometimes they were, when the swell picked up. Occasionally we'd see dolphins and migrating whales. These were charmed moments, but it was brutally hard work herding a drifting flotilla of a dozen beginning kayakers unaccustomed to ocean currents. Often two or three clients would simply run out of gas and we'd have to short rope a few boats together and tow the group home. While the class rarely paddled more than 4 or 5 miles to and fro, Tim and us guides often stroked four times that distance to keep the group from splintering off and drifting into shipping lanes between the coast and Catalina Island. Tim later bought a motorized raft to accompany the group, which made things safer and easier, but for that first summer we were all in kayaks.

By the time we got the group back to shore us guides were so exhausted it took all we had to hose off the boats and load them onto Tim's double-wide trailer. Not so Tim, who worked as hard as a beaver but never seemed to tire. When I asked him about this, he said to meet him the next morning at a greasy spoon breakfast joint in Venice, where I watched him shovel down a prodigious quantity of flapjacks slavered with butter and adrift in a regular lagoon of maple syrup, a four-egg ham omelet, muffins, toast, a pound of fatty bacon, a rasher of hash, pork links, fried spuds, cream horns, etc.

"You guys eat that hippie food," said Tim, burping, "and run outta gas 'cause you ain't got no calories on board."

I'd been onto sports nutrition for a while and could feel my arteries hardening and my heart lugging under the weight and suet of the three "trucker's specials" I'd watched Tim dispatch before my eyes, but I accepted Tim's invitation, powered down two Trucker's Plates my own self and, despite the heartburn, cranked through that day's kayaking tour with ease.

Of course as I learned more about sports nutrition I discovered ways to get the calories without greasy pork links and sugary bear claws, but Tim's point was taken. Big work requires calories. Loads of them. Toast with refried beans and avocado, peanut butter granola, chocolate hazelnut spread, and oatmeal waffles, to mention a few options, deliver the same punch as any old-school American breakfast. Point is, how you get your calories is your business, but get them you must or your body will start cannibalizing itself for the fuel you didn't take on beforehand.

NEVER TOO MUCH FOOD

I've gone on thousands of one- and two-day (weekend) adventures, and rarely if ever do I return home with uneaten food. Keeping fueled up is as important as keeping hydrated. And somebody will always eat what you can't. One time I brought an entire tom turkey with fixings out to Joshua Tree for a one-day climbing trip and only came back with bones. More often than not the moment we hit the highway home we swerve into a restaurant because we're starving after an active day. That kind of beatdown takes a day to recover from. Sure, weight is usually a concern, but however much food you can bear to carry, pack it along and live large.

WILDERNESS FIRST AID

Ongoing education in wilderness first aid is a general requirement for leaders of accredited outdoor programs. Injuries frequently occur in the wild places, and people are left to deal with the skill and knowledge they have—or wait till others arrive who can assist. The problem is the wait. In medical terms, the *golden hour* refers to the period of time following a traumatic injury during which there is the highest likelihood that prompt medical and surgical treatment will prevent death. The Remote is *not* Venice Beach, where lifeguards are constantly scanning the surf and can yank a distressed swimmer from the waves in a matter of minutes as emergency crews converge on the sand. Even on local trails, for example, paramedics are unlikely to arrive in less than an hour.

Extreme adventure sport athletes are the likeliest to suffer serious injuries in the wilds, and they also are the most likely to know nothing about wilderness first aid. I never did during my active years. This is a critical issue that needs immediate attention. More than a few adventurers might not have perished from accidents had those on hand understood even basic first aid. Bottom line is if you're not prepared for accidents, survival in some cases is a crapshoot.

Take a wilderness first-aid class. They are widely available, inexpensive and usually can be completed in a few weekends.

REI has compiled the following list of what a first-aid kit should have:

Basic First-Aid Kit
- Antiseptic wipes (BZK-based wipes preferred; alcohol-based OK)
- Antibacterial ointment (e.g., bacitracin)
- Compound tincture of benzoin (bandage adhesive)
- Assorted adhesive bandages (fabric preferred)
- Butterfly bandages / adhesive wound-closure strips
- Gauze pads (various sizes)
- Nonstick sterile pads
- Medical adhesive tape (10 yard roll, min. 1-inch width)
- Blister treatment
- Ibuprofen / other pain-relief medication
- Insect sting / anti-itch treatment
- Antihistamine to treat allergic reactions
- Splinter (fine-point) tweezers

- Safety pins
- First-aid manual or information cards

This sounds like quite a load, but most of these items are small and light and can be organized into a small nylon bag. Most people simply buy a ready-made kit with a bag designed for that purpose. Make sure to replace whatever gets used before heading back into the wilds.

For multiday trips with groups, the following items are usually added:

- Elastic wrap
- Triangular cravat bandage
- Finger splint(s)
- SAM splint(s)
- Rolled gauze
- Rolled, stretch-to-conform bandages
- Hydrogel-based pads
- First-aid cleansing pads with topical anesthetic
- Hemostatic (blood-stopping) gauze
- Liquid bandage

Expeditions and commercial trips will additionally want some or all of the following:

- Prescription medications (e.g., antibiotics)
- Sunburn relief gel or spray
- Throat lozenges
- Lubricating eye drops
- Diarrhea medication
- Antacid tablets
- Oral rehydration salts
- Glucose or other sugar (to treat hypoglycemia)
- Injectable epinephrine (for severe allergic reactions)
- Aspirin (primarily for response to a heart attack)

AIN'T CHEAP

Look at the old (1924) sepia prints of Mallory and Irvine and marvel at how the English mountaineers, dressed in wool sweaters and tweed coats, ever got 800 vertical feet from the summit of Mount Everest.

Modern outdoor gear is a blessing to use and a curse to buy. A top-end Gore-Tex rain parka, weighing less than eight ounces, costs more than my first *and* second car.

A common refrain within the outdoor world is: *Never pay retail for anything.*

If you can't scam those Smartwool socks, look for sales. Manufacturers continually update their line, so last year's model is plenty good. Popular items can be had for a price because they often are overstocked. A hundred other reasons make it possible to find nearly everything on sale.

I've known thousands of professional outdoors people, and if they don't get stuff for free, or with a pro deal, they buy it out of bargain bins.

DAY PACK

Don't buy a cheap book bag for outdoor use. They're poorly made and fall apart. Get a good one, with minimal pockets and do-dads.

Small technical day packs are great deals because they are basically just nylon, reinforced straps/gear loops, and zippers. Good ones are found on sale for fifty bucks and will usually last ten years if you don't drag them over rocks. They come in all shapes and sizes, and one will fit your style and needs. It's a personal item (like a purse or wallet) that goes wherever you go, so style is a factor for most of us. One pocket for personal items like keys, wallet, and phone, another for stuff you leave in the pack like sunblock, DEET, lip balm, energy bars, and your headlamp, with the big chamber left for clothes and supplies.

Get used to carrying a day pack. For short outings it might be nearly empty, but it's easier to keep stuff secure and organized instead of cramming everything in the pockets of your shorts or pants. That's how stuff gets lost, like keys.

A quality day pack is a companion. It's got your stuff. It's part of you.

TEST DRIVE PACKS AND SHOES

Since we are *wearing* packs and shoes on our bodies, pressure points (ones so subtle you can't feel them when trying on a pack or pair of shoes in the shop) can blister our feet or shoulders in half a mile. Avoid the common mistake of going with a popular brand if the fit is not ideal for you. Some products simply don't feel right, no matter the hype or quality. By whatever means, try to determine what pack or shoe best fits your physique *before* buying. Gear demos are common in both shops and outdoor events, where gear reps have big duffels of products for test drives. Renting (if possible), or trying a friend's gear on for size, is another option. Most packs and virtually all shoes come in various sizes, but no brand or model fits everyone. Fit is the key issue with both items. Even with a glove fit, break that stuff in before any extended use. You can't expect to return gear to shops or manufacturers after you've covered them in mud or worn down the soles, so once you find something that works for you, stick with it till a clearly better product (read: *fit*) comes along. Since gear is ever evolving, a better product *will* come along—of that we can be sure. Find it and use it when it does. Staying old school, fixed in our ways, is like letting our tools collect rust, and putting virtue on doing so. Stay in the mainstream. It pulls us along and keeps us current. A fly in amber can't move.

HEADLAMPS

Even on short outings, *always* keep a headlamp in your pack, removing it only to recharge or swap out batteries. Backup batteries (even for rechargeable units) are likewise standard kit. The benefits of hands-free illumination are as countless as the perils of trying to climb or bike or hike a trail in the dark. Headlamps also help stretch the day, knowing you can climb or cave well after dark and still make it back to your ride. More robust models allow full-on night adventures. When Tommy Caldwell and Kevin Jorgesen free climbed the Dawn Wall, one of the biggest events in adventure sports history, they often climbed at night with headlamps (colder weather means better grip with hands and shoes). Lamps fashioned for mountain biking (some run 400 bucks) are basically head-mounted spotlights allowing bikers to bomb singletracks in the dead of night. Waterproof (to a degree) models won't crap out in a downpour. Leading manufacturers all have a basic model that's also a great deal and works well in most situations.

As it goes with all gear, the basic model will probably take you well onto moderate ground. Intermediate and expert folks will favor specialized lamps for the cold, for wet climates, for situations requiring a tight or narrow or extra bright beam (rated in lumens), with various settings and battery options. Each sport knows best which lamp, at that time, works best for given adventures. Sponsored athletes go with their sponsor's product, but they're always just variations on a proven theme/model. Peer groups and the internet can clue you in on the particulars, which evolve year after year.

That said, lithium batteries are the first choice for cold weather. They're far pricier than alkaline batteries but last much longer in cold conditions. Rechargeable nickel metal hydride (NiMH) batteries also perform well in the cold, but lose power between charges, so carry a few alkalines (excellent at holding their charge) as backups.

BUG OFF!

Mosquitoes, ticks, wasps, gnats, chiggers, hornets, midges, fleas, lice, no-see-ums, bees, horseflies, yellow jackets—these and other pests all eagerly seek a piece of us, nicking a speck of our hide or drilling in for some red stuff, returning the favor with Lyme disease, malaria, dengue fever, west Nile disease, Chikungunya, yellow fever, sleeping sickness, meningoencephalitis, or squeezing out a drop of hellfire that can welt and throb, itch like crazy, even kill some people while causing such aggravation as to drive certain livestock mad. Bug folks (entomologists) swear that insects maintain the balance of life, while the hiker in the Borneo rain forest, machine-gunned by skeeters, or the climber in Java who kicks over the hornet's nest, swears it'd be better just to die.

Like most hazards in The Remote, the key is avoidance, rather than battling bugs on their home court—one reason many favor late fall to early spring (when insects are in far fewer numbers) for extended trips. As summer rounds out, head for higher altitudes. Of course this is impossible for certain adventure sports/events that require long summer days, or when the classic venues are dead center in bug country. Then we have to deal. Here are a few useful strategies.

Slather all open skin with DEET (diethyltoluamide), colorless oily liquid developed by the US Army in 1946 and used widely since the 1980s as an effective insect repellent. The original potion was only good for mosquitoes. Newer DEET-based blends are somewhat effective for a variety of insects. The percentage of DEET in repellent only determines how long the protection lasts. Concentrations of 30 percent offer adequate coverage for up to eight hours—unless you sweat it off, which inevitably happens if you're active.

The verdict is still out per how to best use sunblock and DEET. Some say to first apply sunblock; others say it doesn't matter. Combo sunblock/DEET aerosols receive mixed reviews, especially by manufacturers who sell the ingredients separately. Truth is, after the first doses, further applications, mixing with sweat, fashion a running film that is impossible to keep separated into layers. However you do it, remember that DEET decreases the effectiveness of sunblock by 30 to 40 percent. I reapply both several times a day, as needed. There are non-DEET alternatives, and some sunscreens that are less harmful for the environment, but generally both are less effective, and less popular for that reason. In sensitive areas, like the coral gardens in Costa Rica, environment-friendly sunscreen is required. Once the effectiveness of these products starts to pull even with the more toxic items most of us currently use, they should immediately become required.

Stay covered up, an impossibility when you're active in warm climes, but you can have loose, lightweight garments on hand for any downtime, when the bugs hear the dinner chimes.

If you're just hiking through bug country, go with long-sleeved shirts and long pants, tucked into your socks. Hats also help. Unfortunately for me, the places I've been most tormented by bugs are the jungles and rain forests in South America and the South Pacific, where I'd have perished from heat in full garb. There's no ideal solution for the bug menace, but extended ventures into bug country is true misery without an insect proof tent. I'd rather try to sleep underwater, breathing through a snorkel, then lie out in the jungle getting ravaged by bugs. I've done it, too. Words can't describe the torment.

Ticks are mostly a nuisance—unless they carry Lyme disease, a serious business to be sure. Anytime I'm in known tick areas I stay clear of all brush, grass, and hanging branches because ticks can rub off foliage onto your clothes and skin. I always spray my clothes with Permethrin, a pesticide that kills blackflies, ticks, and mosquitoes but has no harmful side effects on humans. A good practice for hiking partners is to check each other for ticks during every break, and the next time you shower, check every inch of your body, every nook and crease and cranny. I've had several friends go down so hard from Lyme disease that I've made it a thing to avoid tick country if at all possible.

Bugs are a special study and deserve review. DEET and Permethrin are your main repellents, but getting the right combo of clothing and bug juice depends on many factors (temperature and rate of exertion being top of the list). One strategy does not work across the tundra. Read up and experiment. And watch out for ticks. They're heinous.

CELL PHONES

Most smartphones feature GPS navigation, RDS radio receivers, video calling, and more—but none of these work when the battery goes dead. External batteries and portable solar rechargers are helpful, but not if you drop your phone in the stream. That happens, to all of us. For group trips, it's unlikely that everyone's phone will go down, but none are helpful without a signal, which often cuts out in the wilds, especially in canyons and valleys. Guides use cell phones as backup devices. Yes, as primary tools, we always use a headlamp, say, rather than the phone's high-beam light (sucks juice like mad), but who breaks out a map and compass when the GPS and map apps are up and running? Nobody. Just remember, phones break and often go down, so especially for multiday trips, even the best smartphone can never replace navigation skills, physical maps, and reference guides.

LET PEOPLE KNOW WHERE YOU'RE GOING

People often reference the movie *127 Hours* as a reminder to always leave an itinerary with someone near and dear. If nobody knows where we are going, they won't know where to look if we turn up missing. Whoever gets the itinerary must be able to read it. A friend left a map with her mom, with her route highlighted, and her mom had to find someone else who could read the map. Provide an estimated time of return, and always check back in once done, allowing for a big enough time window to allow for weather delays or flat tire—before sending in the troops.

Day Hiking Checklist
- Pick a trail appropriate to your fitness.
- Plan ahead; know the route; check the weather forecast.
- Pack extra food, water, and clothing.
- Go as light as possible.
- Don't rush; take breaks.
- Watch your time.
- Use sunscreen.
- Stop and smell the ponderosas.

Ultralight
Whenever our outdoor experiences move from one day to multiday, we change from outdoor visitors to outdoor travelers. As with all travel, the weight of the stuff we carry becomes an issue, more so than with normal travel because we have to carry everything ourselves. Present-day wilderness travelers carry half the weight for the same trip accomplished even thirty years ago. And with a lot more style and ease. Welcome to the "ultralight" craze, more of a tactic than a product(s). Generic gear lists are helpful as starting points, but so long as we understand the ultralight philosophy, we can dial in the gear according to preference and specific demands.

"Ultralight" concerns both the *weight* and the *amount* of gear we pack into the wilds. Modern gear is light by design, and we don't need much for short excursions. The ultralight MO comes into its own for extended adventures. Four factors figure into the metric of packing what's best for you:

A: Where You Fit on the Performance—Comfort Spectrum
For the person trying to bag Mount Whitney (at 14,505 feet, the highest peak in the Lower 48, and a 22-mile round-trip) say, car-to-car in a day (a fit team can do so in roughly twelve hours), the focus is on performance, and every extra pound matters. A

casual team in "tour mode" might take three days for the same venture. This team favors comfort over exhaustion, and will pack their bag accordingly, taking stuff that would slow the performer. The only "better" in any of this is what best suits your personal style and preference. Whatever you pack, make it light so far as budget allows.

B: Skill Level

No matter the activity, the more you know (skill) the less you need. As you gain experience, you naturally grow more efficient, and as Brendan Leonard succinctly said, "You stop carrying shit you don't need." Ounces mean pounds and pounds mean pain.

C: Fitness

The fit person goes faster and therefore needs less stuff to sustain her over the short term. Or she goes with a pedestrian pace and lugs a few luxuries because she likes them. Fitness gives us options.

D: Grunt Factor

The expert is often willing to schlep a few treats for the pleasure they give. Like gourmet food, actual camera gear instead of just a cell phone, a summit beer, and so forth. Wishing to pay off all that effort, some grunt out a few more pounds. Lighter is not always "more better."

ESSENTIAL GEAR: THE BIG FOUR

Packs. For multiday loads, external frame packs, if used at all, are found mostly on marathon marches (Appalachian Trail, etc.). Virtually everyone else goes with frameless, forty-five- to sixty-liter packs, weighing as little as three pounds. I've always preferred technical packs for big loads. They're sturdier, use better materials, and last longer, and the little extra weight is better than a seam blowing or a shoulder strap ripping out far into The Remote (like the Gulf province of Papua New Guinea). Both have happened.

As a general rule, thirty-liter packs will serve for most day trips. Sixty-liter packs—though not the biggest on the market—will usually serve for trips under a week.

Tents. For trips over two or three days, when rain or weather is expected, tents are required. For shorter trips in fair weather climes, lose the tent and sleep under the stars. Ultralight tarps (most require guylines, trees, stakes, or trekking poles to rig) and bivy sacks (basically waterproof shells) can serve in a pinch for casual outdoors people and are preferred by the hard core.

Sleeping bags. Go with a bag no warmer than you need. Wear socks and a beanie and fleece pullover, and a summer down (much lighter than synthetic fill) bag or even a trekking quilt (favored by thru-hikers) will take you down to moderately cold temps.

Sleeping pads. Self-inflating pads are largely out of fashion. Featherlight air pads are in. Torso-length models are lighter still, though the full-length article is so light that most go with those. That said, many adventurers favor inflatable sleeping pads, which deliver more comfortable sleep (therefore better recovery) for a fraction more weight.

A last word on gear: As with any trend, the ultralight movement comes with its share of bogus gear—either too flimsy, or using ultra high-tech materials at ten times the cost of nylon or aluminum, for example, only to save a few grams. Keeping the weight down is everyone's priority, but an equally key question is *how* you're going to use the gear you have. People on expeditions are hard on gear, and delicate equipment will break in a day. Plastic spoons (a favorite for backpackers) don't cut it during a fifty-day continental crossing of Borneo, for example. You need stuff that will last and can absorb some abuse. You can buy stoves that weigh nothing but use peculiar fuels (hard to replace because they are not widely available) and are fussy to operate, which makes them liabilities when hanging on the side of a mountain with cold hands. Or you cango with an isobutane (canister fuel) stove like a JetBoil, which fires on the first try, but weighs more.

There's generally a tradeoff between durability, ease of use, and weight. Again, what you need depends on how you plan to use it. Ultralight is not the best option in every case. Every trip gives us the chance to review what we took, how critical it was, and to possibly cut down our load for the next adventure.

While "ultralight" is a trend unto itself, minimalism is a solid compass point for all travelers into the wilds.

LAYERING

Since man first invented clothes, we've slipped on layers and peeled them off as we run or linger, while it rains and shines. With the refinement of materials and designs, the ancient art of layering has become a science, enhancing our comfort and safety in The Remote. Layering tiers include a **base layer** (underwear layer), a **middle layer** (insulating layer), and an **outer layer** (shell layer).

Base layers add warmth and keep you dry by moving perspiration away from your skin via "wicking"—essential to avoid chills. Base layers come in cotton, silk, merino wool, polypropylene/polyester, and several lesser-known fabrics. First, a note on cotton.

A cotton shirt will absorb nearly thirty times its weight in water, cooling you down even in warm weather. In moderate cold this is a critical liability. Sweat heavily in cotton and it will soak up and retain sweat, which can chill you as effectively as rolling in the snow. Because cotton traps water inside its fibers, it takes ages to dry. Get a cotton shirt wet in cold conditions and the old motto, *Stay Dry and Stay Alive*, becomes, *Stay Wet and Die*.

In dry, moderate to hot climes, shirts serve as next-to-skin base layers, and cotton remains a favorite. But if there is any chance of getting wet, swap out that cotton for a shirt or pants made from a fabric mentioned below. Anything else is reckless.

Base layers are essentially long underwear (required in moderate to cold temps), though the one-piece Long John is decades gone. Modern articles come in uppers (tops) and bottoms (basically tights). Popular synthetic fabrics include polyester, or poly blends incorporating natural fibers, especially Merino wool. Synthetic garments usually cost less and are more durable than wool, but they don't breathe as well, are not as warm, and stink horribly after extended use.

Although polypro remains an affordable option, Merino wool is the go-to fabric for base layers. This fine-grain wool doesn't itch and feels like a dream on your skin. Merino wool is unique in regulating body temperature through a wide range of climates and activities. Antibacterial and moisture-wicking qualities means it dries quickly and won't produce the gym-sock stink of poly weaves. Base layers come in a lightweight, mid-weight, and expedition weight to cover all climates.

Mid-layer garments, worn *over* any base layer, are predominantly made of nylon and fleece combinations.

Soft shell jackets and shirts are the most versatile mid-layer garments used outdoors. Most are polyester fleece: soft and plush (comfortable), flexible, lightweight, durable, and breathable (so you're less likely to overheat). Fleece wicks sweat and moisture away from the body while letting air circulate through the fibers, dries fast, and insulates even when wet, making it the first choice for outdoor outerwear.

In the 1970s, Malden Mills partnered with outdoor clothing company Patagonia, and together debuted Synchilla fleece—a strong, pile (early fleece) fabric made to imitate wool. The owner of Malden—Aaron Feuerstein—decided not to patent fleece, allowing it to be accessible to the masses and inexpensive to manufacture and buy. Currently, much of the fleece used in jackets and mid-layers comes from recycled plastic bottles and containers, meaning that $200 pullover was only last year so much trash floating in the sea—and that's a good thing.

Fleece coats and pullovers are essential when the weather is unpredictable and we need to layer up, and for several decades have replaced wool as the favored fabric to combat cold. Plus it's warmer, lighter, and usually cheaper than wool. Popular weaves are still modeled on natural wool to achieve a suave, blanket texture. That said, fleece's breathability also means rain and wind whistles right though it as the cold creeps in, so a hard shell outer is required for wet and windy conditions.

Hard shell jackets do what soft shells never can: protect against wind, rain, and snow. Usually coming in one, two, or three stitched layers, hard shells are highly versatile, pack small, breathe well, and dry quickly. Quality shells use waterproof, water-resistant, or windproof technologies, forgoing insulation to keep the weight down. Top-end shells are expensive, but every leading brand has a basic model at a reasonable price, which often is their best-selling item. These are some of the best bargains in the outdoor market and are favored, even among pros, for everyday use.

Insulated jackets use goose down or a synthetic fill to trap body heat. Lightweight insulated jackets ("puffies") pack small and burn hot (amazing weight-to-warmth ratio), though the outer layer is usually a single-layer polyester or nylon face fabric offering little protection against wind, rain, and snow. In dry, cold conditions, they work well as outer layers. In wet conditions they're typically layered over fleece jackets when the temperature drops, with a wind/waterproof hard shell pulled over the puffy. Lose the fleece, or even the puffy, during strenuous work to control sweat buildup and avoid overheating. Layer it all back on during downtime. The strategy is to layer up like an onion, losing or adding "skins" (garments) as your body temp rises or drops.

Insulated parkas basically combine a hard shell with a puffy in one composite mega-coat. Most models are ski and snowboard jackets featuring down or synthetic fill (from a little to a lot), covered by a robust waterproof or water-resistant shell. Quality models are pricey, heavy and unsuited for max exertion when body temp soars. But if you take it off, you're freezing—that's the rub. Insulated parkas trade absolute warmth for the versatility achieved though multigarment layering. But they have their place, and are boons to the ski crowd or for anyone stuck in freezing climes who's not climbing mountains or hauling a sled.

Pants follow the same layering strategy as uppers, though our lower bodies don't overheat and sweat so easily, nor are as sensitive to cold as our cores (torso). This wider heat-cold envelope allows us to often lose the mid-layers and go with specialized outdoor pants, hard shell garments often beefed up at the knees and backside. Nylon and polyester are both synthetic fabrics, but while nylon production is more expensive, it's much more durable and weather-resistant, so is favored for outdoor apparel, especially pants. Thickness ranges from sheer nylon/elastic/spandex blends for fair-weather hiking and adventure sports, to special-order britches used to climb Broad Peak in winter. Versatile, all-around models are serviceable from moderate heat down to nearly freezing. Add a mid-layer and they take us down to zero.

Full-on "smart" expedition pants—basically trouser versions of ski parkas—are also widely available and are crafty fusions of intelligent design and space-age fabrics like breathable, waterproof Gore-Tex and PrimaLoft "featherless" fill. These are highly engineered and have many parts and panels so are costly to manufacture, making them more expensive than an Italian suit. Once you have sights on a pair, search the web for discounts and deals, which goes for every item mentioned on this short list.

GET A SYSTEM

He might be a bow hunter. She might fish sockeye salmon from secret Alaskan rooks. Whoever it is and whatever they're doing, the experienced hand has developed a personal system, a basic way of operating and organizing her personal gear and going about her business. This makes her more efficient and helps to eliminate chance.

The marketplace provides many options for every piece of gear. Over time you'll choose and standardize that gear into your personal system, keeping things the same till you find something better, or a more efficient MO. This way your stuff will reliably perform as expected and you can concentrate on safety and performance.

Someone without a personal system—no matter their skill level—is disorganized and incompetent, always fumbling with unfamiliar gear and needlessly wasting time. Get your stuff squared away. Develop a personal system.

Procedures and protocols involve using the gear in particular ways, and these too have been standardized into generic systems. Take sailboat racing. Without a standardized system known and used by all, it would take ages to raise a sail. The spinnaker goes up quickly because all hands need not ask any questions. They learn a way to do basic actions, and practice doing so till it's second nature. Rote breeds efficiency, and efficiency breeds champions. "Teamwork" derives from this principle.

There are also personal ways of doing things particular to the individual. In climbing, for example, most gear is clipped to gear loops on your harness, and no two people "rack" their gear the same way. Some people prefer the bigger devices up front; others like them toward the back. Some like slings, belay devices, and free carabiners on the left; others like them on the right, or both sides. The point is to arrive at a consistent system, so in a pinch you can instinctively grab stuff that you know is there. If you go clipping stuff on any which way, you're back to fumbling to find what you want, and at some point that will cost you. Making adjustments on the fly is part of the adventure, but without a basic system we have nothing to adjust.

The person who has a personal system knows, in general terms, what she is doing. Otherwise we're just winging it, which results in a junk show more often than not.

PLAN A TRIP OR ADVENTURE

Future trips and adventure exert a gravity that pulls us from the future, imagining us through hump days and putting lightness in our steps because something new, exciting, different, and (fill in the blank) looms somewhere down the trail. The adventure takes shape as we ritualize it—checking dates, making gear lists, buying stuff as needed, perhaps working on techniques in the meantime that hopefully pay off on D-Day.

Take Andrzej—just don't ask me to pronounce that—a Polish national, oil engineer, and big wall climber I meet a few seasons ago in El Capitan meadow in Yosemite Valley. For forty weeks a year Andrzej works on an oil rig in the North Sea, punctuated twice a year by three-week furloughs in the valley, when he flies in and jumps straight onto 3,000-foot-high El Capitan, solo, and typically spends the next ten to fourteen days as a granite astronaut, living on the wall. "Vacation" it's not, at least by most people's definition; and while tastes differ, that future trip or adventure hangs in Andrzej's future like a pole star, giving direction, purpose, and meaning to the occasional dog day beforehand. This is the magic of a plan, a yet-untold story, which, as Borges once said, "eases the passing of time." When the plan unfolds outdoors, it will always have the flavor of being out of this world, our man-made culture where rules and customs make civilized life possible, but which limit and constrict if never escaped. Cabin fever, restlessness, ennui, and the staleness of routine are often cut down to size by a reset outdoors. A future trip can help us remember that today's blues are not a permanent condition.

Plans can also vitalize a week or even a day, helping us focus on otherwise routine, tedious work, knowing that in a few short hours we're meeting friends to tromp up that canyon or blast down that singletrack. The majority of us try to accomplish this reset within the civilized bubble, by attending concerts, lectures, ball games, art galleries. Essential activities to be sure, but rarely can even the best of these zero us out and start us over, as often happens in The Remote.

Spontaneous adventures have their own charm and appeal, but to us outdoors folk, a plan helps make our world go round. Funny thing is that in writing this about making plans, which is little more than stating the obvious, it reminds me I don't have one. To reap the mojo of a plan, you have to actually make one, or else find yourself sitting in a chair writing about it.

Hiking and Trekking Tours

Hikes and treks come in three basic flavors: thru-hikes, out-and-backs, and loops.

Thru-hikes, as originally defined, meant "an established end-to-end long-distance trail with continuous footsteps and completing it within one calendar year." Classic American thru-hikes include American Discovery Trail (6,800 miles), North Country Trail (4,300 miles), Continental Divide Trail (3,100 miles), and Pacific Northwest National Scenic Trail (1,200 miles), to list a few. The Triple Crown of thru-hikes involves bagging the Pacific Crest Trail, the Appalachian Trail, and the Continental Divide Trail, for a total mileage of just under 8,000 miles.

In practical terms, a thru-hike means end-to-end or end-to-ending hiking, whereby you start at Point A and hike "through" to Point B in one continuous push. For the longer marches, many people "section-hike," picking off long stretches when time and conditions allow, then picking the trail back up at the point where they left off. The more adventurous thru-hikes wind through true wilderness areas or no-exit canyons, say, where there's no traversing off to the road and a burger joint. You either go back to where you started (should you bail), or push on through to the end. I lived in Venezuela on and off for twenty years, and we used to do long thru day hikes, bagging giant ridge lines, starting in one city and ending up in another. All such thru day hikes are shuttles, requiring two cars or a pick up. Warning: Always make sure you have your keys for *both* cars. I've got stories about this but am too embarrassed to write them.

Loop hikes are just like they sound. Perhaps the quintessential loop hike is the Tour Mount Blanc, which circles the highest point (15,781 feet) in the Alps via a 105-mile trek featuring 32,800 feet of elevation gain typically done in ten to twelve days. Great thing about loop hikes is that you end back where you started, which simplifies the logistics on multiday adventures. Thousands of loop hikes have been established worldwide and every year afford countless hikers and trekkers an experience of a lifetime.

Out-and-back hikes are the most common form, and unquestionably the finest American article is to hike up to the back side of Half Dome, in Yosemite Valley, climb the cable route to the top of the granite monolith (rising nearly 5,000 feet above the valley and 8,800 feet above sea level, first ascended by George Anderson in 1875, despite reports declaring it "perfectly inaccessible"), then descending the same way back to the valley. The 13-mile round-trip to "The Dome" features 4,800 feet of elevation gain and is a favorite for summer hikers, when hundreds of tourists stream up the cables most every day.

Thru-hikes, loops, and out-and-backs afford endless opportunities for creative combinations and variations. As you gain experience and confidence, start designing your own hikes. Signature ridges, ranges, canyons, and destinations (like waterfalls, etc.) provide ample ground for new adventures. Plan well, pack light, and go do it.

PAY ATTENTION AND LOOK AHEAD

The people most likely to remain unscathed continuously take preventative actions to remain so. This simple principle often goes missing on the Santa Monica bike path a few miles from my house, where I often go for evening rides.

A winding two-lane cement path barely 10 feet wide, with bikers traveling 10 to 20 miles an hour in both directions, can quickly become destruction derby should a rider veer out of their lane or hook an unannounced U-turn at exactly the wrong time, or if a clueless tourist working his cell phone jags onto the path without looking (common). A rider's best defense is not hyper-vigilance. We merely need to relax, look ahead, and pay attention. That includes paying attention to the sometimes foolish comments coming from those whose neck was saved by bikers driving into the sand or braking suddenly or even laying down their bike to avoid impact.

"You're going too fast," some say, wagging a finger at the biker splayed out on the path, road-burned like all get out. "Didn't you see me?" others wonder out loud.

No question, many bikers are as reckless as those wandering onto the bike path while texting. But the point is, when your head's split open on the side of the road, it won't hurt any less or heal faster because you were "right." The entire plot is about avoiding accidents in the first place, and taking an entitled mindset into The Remote, expecting Nature to care about our well-being in any way, is a sure way to find trouble. The mountain or trail or desert takes no account of our well-being. That responsibility falls on us and only us. Early on we often have mentors to keep an eye on us, but little is guaranteed. The Remote is a great teacher in self-sufficiency. But it can strike down the person who expects anything less.

In real-world terms, every time we venture into The Remote we're on our own. Rangers, rescue teams, and conscientious people might come to our aid, but the damage has already been done.

Relax, pay attention, and look ahead.

MISTAKES AND MISHAPS

For over half a century, the most popular publication of the American Alpine Club has been their annual *Accidents in North American Mountaineering*. Ghoulish curiosity? Not hardly. No one lives long enough to learn everything firsthand. Nor would we want or need to. Countless online resources break down accidents and mishaps in exhaustive detail so we don't have to make them ourselves.

MASTERPIECE

Consider pianist Bill Evan's liner notes for "Kind of Blue."

"Miles Davis conceived these settings (musical frameworks) only hours before the recording dates and arrived with sketches which indicated to the group what was to be played. Therefore, you will hear something close to pure spontaneity in these performances. The group had never played these pieces prior to the recordings and I think without exception the first complete performance of each was a take."

If there ever was a field where "practice makes perfect," it's surely music. So how can these players ad-lib a masterpiece? Because the master can find something on the fly that's unavailable through rehearsing. Those favoring structure are often overmatched by works like "Kind of Blue," which require nearly as much from the listener as the man with the horn. Daring listeners, however, will find a magical order in the adventure, when the direction is dead-reckoned and the outcome, at the outset, is unknown by all.

Try, for a second, to imagine planning an adventure travel trip using the format just described. You have a map and a couple sign posts, but beyond that, you simply wing it. Few would consider this the formula for success. So we research a place and start drafting lists to ensure we mine the pay dirt. Only makes sense. The problem: Trying to plan out every minute of your trip from your condo assumes you already know what's best about a place before you get there.

What does "best" or "successful" actually mean here? It almost always refers to visiting places or things of common and proven interest, like cathedrals or peaks or towering redwoods—attractions worth seeing for sure—but when we design our adventure down to the minute, we might, as Brendon Leonard said, "find ourselves behind schedule on our damn vacation."

An adventure, by definition, is an encounter with the unknown, the brand spanking new, at least to us. Sure, we stack the odds that we should encounter the worthwhile, the proven, and the classic, while knowing we likely will share the pleasure with many others. So schedule in enough time to spontaneously explore the unforeseen—the creek not shown on the map; the cobblestone street with the funny name, winding into shadow; the wave breaking off the point in the distance. Why bother? What do we really want if not something to affirm that we're alive, something to give joy, to expand our take on the world and ourselves, to discover untapped resources, to wrangle meaning and value spontaneously and out of midair, to find something immediate that touches us deeply and truly.

You need a plan, but leave some breathing room in your schedule to discover something on the fly, to improvise, to wander around aimlessly. You just might find, not merely a life, but a masterpiece.

GOOD TO KNOW

Early on—I must have been a senior in high school—things went all wrong during a climb on El Gran Trono Blanco, in Baja, Mexico, and I first encountered the mysteries of big danger. Mystery in this regard was not about encountering revealed wisdom or special knowledge, rather operating with a complete lack of it. I didn't *know* anything. I was thrust so far out of my comfort zone that everything felt alien and chaotic, and everything I did felt made up on the spot. The sandblasting winds and rocks falling off the summit were completely out of our control. Hanging in hammocks lashed to the 1,200-foot-high wall, in the middle of the night, we couldn't move and thought we were done for.

There's something magical and insane found in dangerous moments, especially if they're shared with others. Risk we can handle, but no sober person seeks fatal conditions by choice. There's no question that there are those who tend to organize themselves around such experiences. The circumstances come in many flavors, sizes, and shapes: soldiers caught in an ambush, firemen trapped in a blaze, alpine climbers pummeled by avalanche—anyone who makes it through will remember these moments as the most intense, and strangely real moments of their lives. There's nothing macho about it. Hero and coward are meaningless terms referring to people trying their best to survive. Some do better than others, through no choice of their own. At some point in every epic, we usually play every part. Later we regroup to "remember the time." We rarely choose our epics. They seem to choose us. And randomly.

Before my first expedition, to Kalimantan, Indonesia, I was in Frank Morgan's Jakarta bachelor's house, organizing our mountain of gear, and Frank said, "Well, somebody's going to go down because it always happens on these big trips." Then he laughed, looked at me, and said, "Just hope it's you, not me." About thirty days in, expedition organizer Rick Ridgeway, first to climb K2 without bottled oxygen, got typhoid and suffered horribly.

If you keep pushing it hard outdoors, no matter your skill and fitness, an epic will probably find you. There's likely no avoiding it, which is why preparation is so critical, so that when the epic finds you, your survival is never in question. Very few epics are death sentences or anything like it. Sure, there are random acts of God like avalanches and shark attacks, but these are statistically rare. Most people's epics involve a few tough hours or days, which often are greatly lessened if you prepare for the worst and happen to find it. The people who make the headlines are almost always those who were blindsided by events and conditions to which they were unaware. It's not *all* in the preparation. Just mostly so.

It's All on Us

Yosemite climbing pioneer Royal Robbins was once a witness in a lawsuit involving a climber who was injured when a specialized protection device didn't arrest his fall but rather ripped from the crack. The lawsuit sought to blame the accident on the equipment, holding the manufacturer responsible for the climber's broken leg. When an attorney asked Robbins what, in his expert opinion, caused the injury, Robbins pointed to the injured climber and said, "He fell."

Everyone venturing into The Remote is responsible for their own safety. That was Robbins's point. Climbing is inherently dangerous. So is every adventure sport. Injuries from "acts of God," like lightning and rockfall are statistically rare, and even these are often avoidable if you know the conditions where they commonly occur. Expecting equipment to save us attempts to shift responsibility to the gear we use, which can foster a mindset of expecting equipment to counteract dangerous terrain and decisions. The truth is, the only way to eliminate all risk is to never leave the house.

Our margin of safety derives from where we choose to go and the decisions we make when we go there. These are largely under our control. Modern gear increases our potential safety, but what matters is how we use it.

If we hike below a rumbling bergschrund, get buried under an avalanche, and our beacon gets crushed in the process, it's not the beacon's fault if we perish. At best the beacon might have saved us from the results of a bad decision, or sometimes even an act of God, but it is never the beacon's "fault" either way.

Most of us never venture into danger zones where acts of God are remotely possible. When we take responsibility for our own safety, we naturally stay alert to potential hazards. Dozing on the job, or expecting our gear to save us no matter what, is a good way to discover if it will, and there are no guarantees in that regard.

If you're traveling into danger zones like mountains or avalanche prone areas, into malarial jungles, deep water caves, canyons during the rainy season, or if you're chasing technical adventure sports, accept that there's a long learning curve requiring training and education, mentors, and serious immersion so the dangers are known and understood. Then some years working up the ladder. Accident reports are full of peole who tried to shortcut the process. That's not a warning. It's a fact.

"Acceptable risk" assumes that the person knows what those risks actually are, and this is always an inexact science owing to so many variables, especially weather. Experienced hands factor in a certain margin of error for what we expect and plan for.

Process

THE FUN SCALE

Simply being outdoors has birthed everything from hammerstone petroglyphs to *plein air* painting, where an artist escapes the four walls of the studio and sets to work in the landscape. If all the outdoors is a stage, where's the glory in standing around doing nothing? In modern times we see this dynamic in outdoor recreation, writ loud and large with the exploding adventure sports movement. We hike up hills and bike down trails and paraglide and climb and surf and spelunk. This is how many of us find our way outdoors, through activities and outing groups.

Every outdoor pursuit has a laundry list of particulars. Memorizing the dive tables won't much help the skier, but some basics apply to any outdoor activity, orienting principles that apply across the tundra. One of these is the Fun Scale, created to try to gauge the gravity of outdoor adventures, though the scale itself mirrors the currents of life, flowing between bliss and agony.

Type 1 Fun

Pure fun. Fun to plan, fun while it's happening, and especially fun to remember. Type 1 fun seems too good to be true, how the stars aligned and our plans came together so handsomely. Low risk, low commitment, moderate effort, perfect weather, and selfies all around. One definition of utopia is "there is no such place." Whoever said so never had Type 1 fun.

Type 2 Fun

Type 2 fun is a strange beast, never fun to do but rewarding to remember. It might be hateful start to finish, though it likely won't kill or maim you. Type 2 fun refuses to be over. You have to push on, feeling anxious, clumsy, overmatched. *What was I thinking?*

Type 1 fun can morph into Type 2 with no warning. It snows—*in July*. Your kayak paddle snaps three strokes into the canyon. The rope gets stuck, and life goes sideways from there. Writer Tim Peck said that you celebrate Type 1 fun with pitchers of beer, while Type 2 fun "leaves you feeling like you *need* a drink." Most "No Shit, There I Was" stories derive from Type 2 fun.

The dragon slayers in any adventure sport are captivated by Type 2 fun. Most of them were born with a character that only finds completion on the edge. One motto for this group is, "It doesn't have to be fun to be fun." Don't try to figure that out because even they can't. It's nothing you can learn. Like being born with freckles, you come to like it if you can. Don't let the smiling cover shots fool you. No dragon slayer escapes unscathed.

Every World Cup downhill racer has crashed and rag-dolled down a mountain at 80 mph. Every big wave surfer has suffered a two-wave hold-down, clawing to the light and yelling for their mother. The world-class adventurer is skilled and resilient (and more than a few are held together with rivets, plates, and duct tape), but continued success owes less to heroic resolve than a gift for forgetting.

No one slays dragons forever. Ten years is a great run, and you never get that far without a porous memory, forgetting the toils by focusing on the next big project. I chased dragons for as long as I possibly could, till life caught me from behind, and finally I forgot how to forget. For everything its season.

Type 3 Fun

Type 3 fun is supposed to kill you, yet somehow didn't. It's a sufferfest from hell, a Homeric epic. You were lucky to survive, and the experience will haunt you to the cooker. If you get out with all your toes and fingers, you're blessed because we usually pay for big mistakes in the outdoors. Type 3 fun entirely lacks poetry.

One of the curious rituals we humans perform is intentionally staging events that appear—at least to us spectators—as Type 1 fun, but can result in Type 3 train wrecks in a flash.

The need to encounter a looming and fatal threat, if only by proxy, is lodged in our DNA. The catharsis delivered through the threat of Type 3 debacles is needed most by the person believing they've transcended primitive impulses. Such a person is fussy, anal, and drinks too much, fixated as they are on control. We all get that way at times—till someone drags us to a nude beach or a NASCAR race and we scream and laugh our way back to sanity—and Type 1 fun.

I vividly recall when bull riding world champion Lane Frost took on Red Rock, the legendary 1,750-pound, red brindle bull, in "The Challenge of the Champions." Red Rock had 307 outs (trips out of the bucking chute) with no qualified rides, and looked likely to become the only bull in rodeo history that would retire unridden. A legend was born when, after two failed attempts, Frost rode Red Rock to the eight-second horn.

The next year, during Cheyenne Frontier Days, Frost had just dismounted after a successful ride on a bull called Takin' Care of Business. He landed on hands and knees in the mud just as the bull turned and gored him with his right horn in the back, breaking some ribs and severing an artery. Lane Frost died in that arena.

The far side of the Fun Scale is often survived but never conquered.

The outdoors is a big enough stage to accommodate all types and flavors of fun, but in our collective consciousness, the Fun Scale is imaginary as each of us plays every part—if only in our dreams.

Pay Attention

In 1989, at a small crag in France, Lynn Hill forgot to finish tying her knot connecting the climbing rope to her harness. At the top of a 70-foot warm-up, she started to lower off the anchor on top; the unsecured rope end pulled through her harness and Lynn went airborne, windmilling her arms to stay upright. She crashed through branches of a tree and piled into the ground between two boulders, miraculously sustaining only a dislocated elbow and a broken ankle.

When Lynn first told me about this accident, perhaps a year after it happened, I wondered how the many-time World Sport Climbing champion, the visionary who had first free climbed *The Nose* (on 3,000-foot-high El Capitan, Yosemite Valley), and my longtime partner on and off the cliffside, had made such a rookie mistake. Twenty-five years later, at a climbing gym 3 miles from my house, I also failed to finish the tie-in knot to my harness. The last thing I remember after reaching the chains at the top of the route is landing feet first on the ground, crumpling in a heap and rolling up to see my tibia jutting out a hole in my shin. Fifty days and five operations later, I got discharged from UCLA Medical Center and spent most of the next year on crutches.

In the long months following my accident, I felt puzzled and humiliated that Lynn, possibly the world's finest free climber in the early 1990s, and I, who'd climbed steadily for forty years and had written a dozen books on technical climbing, had both fallen asleep on the job. I felt especially guilty having decked in the "safe" environment of a climbing gym. A little research showed that while serious gym accidents are rare (occurring less frequently then hill walking, for instance), they *do* happen, the majority of which are basic pilot error.

The question was: How did we, with decades of experience between us, simply fall asleep? The answer became clear when I read an article about industrial safety protocols, subtitled: "Complacency is Safety's Worst Enemy." This is especially so outdoors, where conditions constantly change. "Shit happens" in the wild, and not only to adventure sports athletes.

No matter the adventure, we never get far without basic skills. More often than not, the skill that brings us home is vigilance. The key is to know how vigilance is practiced outdoors, when it goes missing, and why.

Vigilance assumes three basic forms: 1) appraising difficulties, 2) regular reminders, and 3) oversight.

Appraising Difficulties

Experienced outdoors people constantly appraise potential hazards, and discuss solutions as a matter of course. Between waves, surfers talk to each other about shifting tides, peaks, and currents. You'll see some version of this ritual in most every outdoor pursuit and every sport. The champion studies their opponent. We can't appraise the difficulties unless we see them, and we can't see them unless we're paying attention.

Regular Reminders

A safety checklist, part of every sport and outdoor activity, is not a one-time drill. We repeat it over and over, reminding ourselves of what to avoid, and checking our own systems at regular intervals. That's the reason cars have gauges, which inform us about current conditions. We know those conditions will change over time, introducing a new set of potential hazards.

Double-checking our systems, glancing at our "gauges" during every lull, is part of our standard practice. Anything less is driving with our eyes closed. When we try that on the freeway, it's dangerous and terrifying. Complacency is when our eyes are closed but we're not scared. In the ways that matter, we're asleep.

Oversight

Oversight means not only checking our own systems, but also that of our partners, recognizing hazards and mitigating them. The experienced day hiker tromping up the well-worn path will see and give notice about the gravelly wet section at the jag in the switchback. Hit it unawares, and even the Swiss mountaineer goes down.

Many are injured doing basic procedures they've done a thousand times—because they got complacent. Scores of climbers have perished in rappelling accidents, one of the simplest drills in the sport. Half of the rescues in Yosemite are for people who hiked off the trail. Most of the others happened when the hard part was over and people let their guard down. These are not just rookie mistakes. The best of us get complacent. Fighting complacency is a team effort. Without constant vigilance, the wilds have the advantage.

Remember the old mountaineer's motto: The most critical part of the whole shebang is the next 10 feet.

LEARNING TO LEARN

Recall those people deaf from birth who are fitted with a surgical implant that allows them to hear for the first time, but the stimulus is so foreign and chaotic they often hit the OFF switch. When we're overmatched we don't have the expert's library of experiences to draw from. We can't recognize the details. We drown in a river of stimulus. That was me when I first started mountain biking and headed down a technical singletrack, all the details blurring together in a cascade of unknowns. I was trying too much, too fast. I couldn't learn anything. I was just trying to survive, making every mistake possible, even inventing a few when slamming into ruts and rocks and the bars were ripped from my hands, sending me flying. I had to find some easier terrain.

It took me little time to learn mountain biking basics once I left my expert friends and started puttering around on pedestrian trails. As soon as I developed some little feel for the work, I could get out of my own way and let my body learn how to execute while paying attention to the overall process. The rest happened largely on its own.

No matter the activity, learning happens when we slow the process down, even stop before the hard bits, gathering ourselves and letting our minds unboggle. Slowly we become aware of what formerly was a blur, growing conscious of details, how our body is positioned, and so forth, making adjustments as required instead of face-planting into the dirt.

Learning has its own rhythm, which is interrupted by impatience and pushy coaches. Solid skills are built on fundamentals. Rush through those and your foundation is so much sand. You'll quickly dead-end and have to start over again, unlearning a slew of bad habits. It's worth noting that when a professional slumps for unknown reasons, they often return to the basics and work forward from there.

FINDING IT

Renowned 1930s-era golf pro Stewart Maiden had an interesting approach to teaching, which, according to two-time Masters champion, Ben Crenshaw, "was simple and direct, avoiding all technicality." Not to say Maiden's coaching didn't improve a player's technique, just that he never tried to standardize a golf swing into "ideal" or preferred parts, believing you could no more do so than you could break a great song down to notes, and there's more than one great song, besides.

General principles are always in play, like "keep your eye on the ball" and "take dead aim." But golfers—and all of us doing adventure sports—come in so many shapes and sizes that trying to impose a one-style-fits-all approach never brings consistently good results. *Maiden's Law*, as we might call it, is accepting that a player's natural style is their best asset, and that improvement is quickest and most effective through augmenting, rather than directly changing, that style. The question is *how?*

In terms of action sports, the surfer who relies mostly on power is coached to relax and *find* "the silk" (smooth elements) in her movements. The mountain biker relying on balance and flow works on finding punch and explosive force in his riding, and to find a touch more. And so forth. By adding small, organic condiments to the athlete's natural style, people improve in ways impossible using other methods.

Within any given style are elements of every style. That was Maiden's basic insight. No one surfs, paddles, climbs, and so on without some measure of balance, touch, flow, power, flexibility, agility, and quickness. Even the most spasmodic skier has *some* silk in her movements. The moment she finds it and *feels* it, her jerky style naturally smooths out. Likewise, there is latent power in the "weak" surfer who relies on agility, flexibility, and fluid movement, and once he finds that power, taps it, and consciously lets it rip, more power naturally follows.

Cross-training weaknesses is helpful, but the training is most meaningful after a person finds the underdeveloped element already working in their physical experience. Initially, the difficulty might have to be dialed back for a person to fully realize how a latent skill is already present in their game. When an Olympic lifter, say, starts adding a new wrinkle to their technique, they first drop down the weight to get the hang of it. Once the process begins, practice is much more focused and intentional, and the dividends just keep coming.

J. B. MAUNEY

Some years ago I covered the George Paul Memorial Bull Riding Challenge, "The toughest rough stock even in tarnation." I spent the first evening with Jim Sharp, current world bull riding champion; Tuff Hedeman, former champion; and Ty Murry, many time overall champion. Sharp had a home gym that looked like Muscle Beach, Venice. These guys were fit.

When the bull's-only rodeo kicked off the next day, I was an instant believer that bull riding was as advertised: "The most dangerous eight seconds in sport." You better believe it when a bronc lashes himself to the back of a rearing, stomping, 1,800-pound chunk of rump roast from hell. The acrobatic moves these rank bulls perform in their fury to eject the rider has to be seen to be appreciated. Man against beast—adventure sports don't get much rowdier than that.

Maybe a decade later I watched a YouTube video on the current bull riding champ, J. B. Mauney, titled "The Best Bull Rider of All Time." Action footage was garnished with confessionals from J. B.'s friends and fellow competitors.

"There's not a bull in the world that he believes can buck him off," said one old coot, "not a title in the world he don't think he can win."

"Come to him naturally, you know," said another. "It's in the blood . . . in the body. He's just a dirty rotten tough cowboy."

"J. B.'s one of the strangest guys," added a third, "so far as what works for him as a bull rider. He don't work out none. He's scrawny. Only weighs like 140 pounds."

A fourth bronc, shaking his head, summed up the common sentiment: "Comes so easy to him."

Comes easy. He didn't work out. His talent was in his blood. He was champ because he was dirty rotten tough. Perhaps all this was true—but in a sport as technical as bull riding, champions are not made through accident or toughness. Massive preparation is always involved. I filed the confessionals under "Highly questionable."

A few years later I saw another clip of J. B. Mauney inside a barn, standing/balancing on top of a fully inflated basketball, his legs and hips making all the twitchy micro-adjustments, his hands waving the air like a tightrope walker. His face and arms were pouring sweat, his shirt just as soaked as a dishrag.

"Balance, for me, is a huge part," said Mauney. "It doesn't matter how strong you are, you'll never outmuscle a damn 1,800-pound bull. Standing on this ball, the way it rolls, the way you have to move your weight, it's just like a bull. If I don't have anything to do, I'm in here, standing on the ball. A lot of them, they tell me,

'You're a freak of nature.' But they're not in here. I let them think what they want to."

That same year I was over in Switzerland (where skiing is religion) and saw a World Cup skier trying to stand on a hard rubber, basketball-sized exercise orb. He could barely stay up there for three minutes before his legs started shaking and he'd topple off. Your core is engaged the whole time, your legs are flexed, your calves screaming for mercy. Eventually you seize up and topple off, even a downhill racer. Our boy J. B. had worked up to staying on the ball thirty times longer than a pro skier.

The point here is not a basketball, but the mindset Mauney developed to find and use it like he did.

J. B. stepped outside the bubble of conventional wisdom that said a successful bull ride hinged on toughness, desire, and strength, and that while balance was certainly a factor, you couldn't work on that, or your native toughness, so you work on other factors, especially strength. Since all top bull riders were young, fit, and strong, strength differences between them amounted to nothing to a one-ton bull. Balance was the issue, and J. B. found a way to train it that translated directly to bull riding.

Advances are made when someone discovers a new approach to an old practice. An update that builds on the past but differs in ways that matter. It was taking the wide view, seeing what was actually involved, and finding a solution that directly addressed the challenge.

I never thought for a second that J. B. Mauney was merely tough.

LEADERS AND DECISIONS
(From conversations with kayaker Jeff "Pork Pie" Flynn)
I want to kayak Linville Gorge, in North Carolina—some of the fiercest whitewater in America. The "Grand Canyon of the East." And I want to go to the High Sierras and climb the *Mountaineers Route* on Mount Whitney, the classic scramble/climb on the

highest summit in the continental United States. And I want to bow-hunt wild bores on Catalina Island. Just because. I could list one hundred different adventures, and the decision-making process, and the subtle traps awaiting me, remain largely the same.

This time we're paddling the Linville Gorge. Pork Pie Flynn put it this way.

"I hit up five of my favored partners, people I trust. Three say *no* straight off. Linville Gorge is Class V. People drown down there. Not a river for everybody. One of the two remaining partners, Joe, is all in; the second, Danny, is on the fence. How do I handle Danny?

"Back in my teens and early twenties, whenever one of us got some hare-brained notion to swim the Colorado River through the Grand Canyon (Bobby Kennedy did most of it) or climb the volcanoes down in Mexico, we'd bum rush potential partners as though they had no choice but to sign on. Immediately. Pity the fool who scoffed or hedged. We'd badger and shame the guy till he finally agreed, just to get us to shut up. If there's a worst strategy, I don't know it.

"As a semi-conscious adult, I never advise what decisions my partners should make, especially when I feel like it. The urge to do so—I heard somewhere—comes from wanting to manage other people's lives, which I might chalk up to being an effective leader, while in fact I'm a selfish con who's full of himself and who's asking for trouble besides.

"But say I do strong-arm Danny into joining Joe and I on the Gorge, goosing Joe's enthusiasm to enlist Danny via peer pressure. That's the first bad move. When people make a decision under pressure, it's likely the wrong one. And if Danny goes down, Joe and I are on the hook. It matters little that others might not know we shanghaied Danny onto the Linville. His misfortunes, whatever they are, will hang around my neck, and I don't want that. Only if Danny is compelled to make his own decision can the team enter the Gorge 'clean.'

"Rule of thumb: A good leader doesn't make personal decisions for others. Ever. Rather she inspires people to develop the strength, character, and experience to work things out for themselves. If you drag someone along without these qualities, especially when the adventure requires big skills, you're opening the door for disaster epic.

"What happens, say, if halfway through the Gorge, Joe, and I get injured and can't continue under our own power? Not everyone has the strength of purpose to take decisive action. If Danny is thrust into a position of working things out for the whole team, what if he can't? Note that top-drawer alpinists try always to have partners who can take charge anywhere on the mountain. They often have to. If your go-to person has been dragged there by the short hairs, and folds under pressure, you've forgotten the golden rule in The Remote: 'shit happens.' If you've built the wrong team to handle that, you're not a leader, but a reckless liability to yourself and others.

"These principles apply just the same once we paddle into the gorge. Say Danny charges through most of the big water on the Linville, but holds up at Cave Rapid, with its big drops over wash rocks. Should he give it a go, or portage his boat around? Joe and are I right to encourage Danny—if he likes his chances. But the decision to go or not go must be his own. Indecision is poison for big adventure challenges. You need a clear mind and enough confidence to take risks. If those are missing, the only advice I ever give is to bail. The river's not going anywhere.

"Even small adventures fail, with surprising frequency, because we've made selfish and reckless decisions, leaving us with the wrong men and women for the job. Enlisting friends who are overmatched by the immediate challenges is rash and dangerous. You get people hurt that way. Successful adventures, especially risky ones that stretch our limits, need all hands on board, each hand ready and able to lead, as needed.

"It sounds simple, too obvious to mention, but how often it's ignored: When the going gets tough, *a team prevails by willing and able partners.* Enough said."

PACK EVERYTHING YOU THINK YOU'LL NEED, THEN DUMP HALF OF IT

Rule: Pack only the stuff you *need* and are *certain to use.*

Need is determined by your aim, what you plan to do. If you're bird watching, lightweight binoculars are a boon, but if you don't need binoculars, don't pack them. Someone hunting quail doesn't need an elephant gun. That's the strategy in a nutshell.

Know your gear. When deals are found and there's money to spend, replace the heavy stuff with lighter items that often are better performers.

Whatever you can share, do so. A minimal first-aid kit brings peace of mind, but you'll only *need* one for the group. Same goes for maps, etc.

Food and water are usually the heaviest items you'll carry for day adventures. Load up on fluids before you start and consume whatever you take as you go, so your load keeps getting lighter. Ideally you finish with no water and no food. Experience will show you how to shave down the margins.

Check the weather and pack accordingly. You don't *need* storm gear for a summer hike in the Santa Monica Mountains, but you might want a lightweight rain parka for hiking in Maui because it dumps most afternoons. Some people don't. They hike in nylon boardshorts and tech T-shirts (fast-drying nylon blends). It's 65–75 degrees, so who cares if you're wet. Some do, ergo the rain gear.

Warmth is achieved through layering, best achieved with multifunctional garments like a Gore-Tex parka that is both warm and waterproof. Down is lighter for parkas, but costs more. An insulated vest is a good, lightweight option for moderate cold.

In many cases, it's not so much the cold but the windchill factor that gets us pulling on layers. A popular option is a windshirt, which weighs nothing, provides protection and warmth, and allows for lighter base layers.

Most of the luxuries we think we might want, rarely if ever get used, and what we actually need is often little. A common motto is: "Pack everything you think you'll need, then dump half of it."

GEAR WORSHIP

Remember the scene where Ebenezer Scrooge, all alone and hunkered in a cold, drafty cubical, is slumped over a stack of coins, counting, candle flickering as he feels the gold pieces in his hands, as though the coins were talismans, or possessed some hidden value beyond a means of bartering for stuff we want or need.

Gear worship is the outdoor version of Scrooge's fixation on money *in and of itself.* To the extent that gear manufacturers promote their products as anything but a means to the end of selling experiences outdoors, they are wingmen for Ebenezer Scrooge.

Respecting your gear, keeping it ordered and in good condition ensures that it will perform as needed. The operative word is "perform." Outdoor gear, however artful and stylish, is meant to be used. Sure, who hasn't examined their skis during August heat, dreaming of powder, or re-racked their climbing gear in mid-week to evoke the mojo, but when we start purchasing gear just to have it, and avoid using those boots, say, because we're afraid to get them muddy, we mistake the lamp for the magic.

COMMON MISTAKES

My friend Cindy Goldberg has led backpacking trips for twenty years and lists the following as the most common mistakes made in the outdoors:
- Bad or no planning
- Not checking the weather; ignoring storm signs
- Not setting a turn-back time (getting caught in the dark)

- Using unfamiliar, untested gear (especially shoes)
- Forgetting sunscreen and bug juice (when needed)
- Taking shortcuts (and getting lost)
- Getting separated
- Not looking up and ahead (and head-butting stuff)
- Bad pace (going too fast or too slow)
- Not taking breaks ("refuel and recover")
- Not enough warm clothes
- Lugging a big-ass first-aid kit
- Too little water and food
- Forgetting toilet paper
- Taking needless gear
- Going with knuckleheads
- Leaving a trace ("Pack it in. Pack it out. *Always.*")

FINISH WHAT YOU START

Before we had money for gear and a car to drive to proper climbing areas, a couple friends and I spend countless afternoons at Mount Rubidoux, a bushy knoll near Riverside, California, covered with quartzite boulders, where we exhausted ourselves pawing up the small crags and learning the basics. I was jazzed but impatient. If a pesky crack or knobby face gave me problems I moved on to something I could immediately do. Then we met Paul Gleason, a skilled climber who had a knack for basic principles as they related to the outdoors. Paul later became a seminal player in the development of wildland firefighting techniques, basically inventing "the science of fire." His efforts and leadership saved many lives, probably including our own.

Paul knew our little group would go on to bigger things, but if we practiced quitting, quitting would become our style. It didn't much matter at Rubidoux, he said, but on the big walls that we dreamed about, quitting was not always an option.

Finish what you start. Even 10-foot boulder problems. Don't leave till you do it. Then do it again for good measure. That was Paul's way, and we made it our own long before we found ourselves high on a mountain or rock wall, with retreat cut off for many reasons, when the only way off was up. We'd trained ourselves to finish, so we did.

This strategy is relevant to all things outdoors because even on pedestrian terrain, we can't always have our own way. All of a sudden, Nature can impose conditions that we are forced to deal with. If we're used to bailing whenever we want, what happens when we can't?

Take the time I was hiking with my daughter on a popular tourist trail in eastern Venezuela. We'd joined a local hiking club, Dioses Del Rastro (trail gods), which most members used as a means of walking off hangovers. Though a destination (a distant ridge, say, or a waterfall) was usually our stated goal, the group rarely ever got there and instead turned back whenever they felt like it. No harm in that. Being slaves to an itinerary is itself a trap that kills spontaneous exploration, and can force people on when it's better and wiser to bail, or simply stop, meld, and drop to zero. This is an especially important point for anyone raised on instant gratification and overscheduled childhood activities.

There's a downside as well, and it happened when my daughter and I and the trail gods had ventured a few miles down a well-traveled trail and a sudden thunderstorm turned into a two-hour deluge that had us hunkering under trees as the streams we'd crossed getting there swelled into regular torrents. We couldn't reverse course without drowning, and the only way out was to keep charging down the trail till it spilled out at the fringe of a little pueblo 6 miles away. Having little to no experience pushing themselves as conditions sometimes require, the trail gods were initially vexed that they couldn't bail at will. So with much cursing and moaning we tromped for the distant pueblo. Not surprisingly, through discovering grit few had ever called on, reaching the road was a revelation for most of the crew, whose excursions took on new purpose ever after.

We never know how far we can go till there's no other choice. It's not a method to live by, but anyone who spends time in the wild places will eventually have no other choice. As renowned Yosemite adventure photographer Tom Evans said about the trials of peak bagging in the valley, "That's just the way it is."

HAVE A TARGET

One time I was mountain biking with a small group of friends in the hills above Pacific Palisades, where a vast web of meandering fire trails and singletracks converge at a place called "The Hub." Perhaps 10 miles away, the renowned Mullholland Drive turns into a dirt road/fire trail that rolls straight through The Hub before winding another 20 or so miles and dumping out near the ocean several miles past Malibu. It's hard to get lost on the Mullholland trail, but the dozens of arteries spilling off The Hub are confusing, even with a GPS. Take the wrong fork and you might have to pedal 15 miles before breaking out onto a highway. I know because I've done it. Twice. And both times we took a trail that looked interesting, not exactly sure where we were headed. All roads don't necessarily lead to Rome.

You don't shoot a gun into the air. You shoot at a target. That's the point: hit the target. The target gives the shot meaning. This doesn't preclude changing your target as conditions demand or merely on whim. But striking out without a target is best reserved for short forays off your chosen route, and a chosen route always has a target.

For day hiking, the target is our destination. Without a destination, we don't know where we're going. The destination does not provide all the meaning to a hike. The wilderness does. Our partners do. What a destination *does* mean is that so long as we have one, we're far less likely to get lost.

The target might only be a given trail, or a trailhead offering various paths we can venture down as far as we choose. But once we're done, the trailhead becomes the target, and we better know where that is and how to get there.

Having a target is the best way of keeping track of where we are. It's not the end-all—until we get lost. A common misconception is that in this age of GPS, we're never really lost. With tracking devices, cell phones, and nearly ubiquitous internet access, we pretty much always know where we are—and where we're going. That is, until your signal goes missing for 1,000 reasons, something we've all experienced. During your first trip to an area, unless you're traveling with locals, it's best to have a target *and* a map.

NOT EXACTLY

One time out at Joshua Tree (which everyone calls "Josh"), in Southern California's high desert, a bunch of us hiked out to Barker Dam and were snooping around Bill Keys's long abandoned Desert Queen Mine, a ruin of adobe buildings, rusting car chassis, and the gutted remains of a stamp mill. In May 1942, right there at the Desert Queen, Keys had argued over a mining claim with neighbor Worth Bagley, who pulled a pistol, according to Keys, who then blew Bagley's brains out with a shotgun. Keys was convicted and sent to San Quentin—but that's another story.

On the hike out we ran into a guy sitting on a rock by the mouth of one of the many side canyons and draws between the turnout on the road and the mine. The hike to Desert Queen was only a couple miles, but to someone inexperienced with the area, or with desert travel in general, the Josh outback is a labyrinth.

"You lost?" one of us asked, and the guy, who introduced himself as Mark, said, "Not exactly." We all chuckled, including Mark.

Davy Crockett reputedly said, "I've never been lost, but I'll admit to being confused for several weeks." But after several weeks of confusion in those canyons and draws, dry as Sahara sand, even

Davy Crockett would be as dead as Worth Bagley. Sad to say, but it happens every year to those who go unprepared.

Know where you are and where you're going, or The Remote will bleach your bones.

COURAGE

A friend recently screened a video of three women cave diving in Mexico and said he had to hit the pause button after a few minutes because it gave him "terminal claustrophobia," and he'd never have the courage to go diving in such a dark and enclosed space. "Like swimming around in a big coffin," he said.

The point missed here, as commonly happens, is that the video shows only the final product, three experts plying their craft deep inside a Mexican river cave. What it doesn't show is the decade (at least) run-up to their performance. Chances are that early on, all three started snorkling around their parents' swimming pool, later took up free diving in lakes or in the ocean, got certified in SCUBA, logged hundreds if not thousands of dives in every imaginable condition, slowly got into cave diving, spent years getting the training and certification, and from there, started in tiny little sinkholes, got mentored by experts, read everything possible on the subject, and only slowly worked their way into the liquid bowls of monster caves. The final product, what my friend saw on the video, was preceded by years of training, calculated study, and obsessive practice and preparation.

It's certain that all three divers would have felt "terminal claustrophobia" from being in that cave had they gone there with no training.

None of us can truly picture ourselves performing high-end adventure sports with no background whatsoever in same. That's judging the final product based on our own experience, and when we have none, all we have are the willies. It takes courage to cave dive, even for those at the top of that game, but as the old adage goes, "The greater part of courage is to have done something before."

Magic Days

We've all have "low gravity" days when everything feels effortless. When we move in a charmed bubble, and whatever our activity, it plays directly to our strengths, as if skiing or biking or surfing were invented just for us. Such days are rare for everyone. They demonstrate our potential, and hint at what is humanly possible.

We naturally think in causal terms: What made that day so good? If we can discover the cause, maybe we can replicate our performance and walk among the clouds once more.

Trying to rebuild magic by way of parts is doomed to failure, because if anything earmarks magic, it's how the individual things we did were elements of a unified process. The whole shebang is "of a piece."

When recalling a magic day, the whole gestalt comes back to us as unbroken experience, which carries with it a felt sense. Merely remembering that day evokes trace elements of that felt sense imprinted on our psyche at depth. That's the exercise: Before every time out, *reflect back to a magic day and tap the felt sense of it.* No one can tell you exactly how to do it, but most people can work out a method through trial and error. With practice, evoking this felt sense only requires about thirty seconds to be effective.

Our brains are adept at carrying out instructions, and that's the frame of mind we adopt when we sense back into magical times of peak performance. We're not hoping or asking ourselves to rediscover the magic. We're gently telling ourselves to bring it on, to induce what we already know. When this becomes our ritual, we ride a magic carpet. We can't always find it, but it's always worth the effort when we do.

Projecting

A *project* is not a task in the everyday sense—like painting a room or building a shed. An adventure project is a big deal because it's often the next step, possibly an achievement that crowns our career up to that point. Projects mean upping our game in terms of effort, skill, and commitment. For weekend warriors, it often means learning new skills or refining the ones we have. Projects are not limited to adventure athletes pushing the performance envelope. A hiker or backpacker, say, can fashion projects that are as personally meaningful and rewarding as the podium is to the World Cup skier. For both the pro and the weekend warrior, *the science of projecting* is basically selfsame, and increases our odds at succeeding. Here are a few steps:

Objectify the Venture. Basic information gathering. What is involved, start to finish, and what are the specific demands? Why do people fail or succeed? And so forth.

Cast a wide net. Talk to whoever knows. Read magazine and web articles, and especially trip reports. Get a general feel for the project and decide if it's right for you.

Commit to the Project. If a project hooks you in, commit to *exploring the possibility of doing it.* Develop an action plan so day trips/adventures work toward your project, at the exclusion of what does not. Practice what you hope to play.

Evaluating and Working on Weaknesses. What do you need to develop to bag the project? Often it's a matter of more of the same, meaning endurance. We might have put in long days on the trail or on the rock, for example, but never for a month (for a long thru-hike) or a week (for a big wall climb), as need be. Incrementally work toward your goal, bringing weaknesses up to speed on smaller ventures that simulate the project. There often are tutorials for the classic projects: *The Road to Hiking the John Muir Trail*, and so forth.

In short: Learn what you're in for; evaluate your skillset; objectively work toward your goal, shoring up weaknesses on tasks resembling the project.

Timetable. Once you commit and start working toward a project, your progress will determine a future date to aim for. Give yourself a window, but set a target date, basically a deadline, without which much of the world's work would never get completed.

Timing. Weather-dependent projects might entail short holding patterns if it's snowing, say, or even if you're not "feeling it," but avoid lengthy delays. Enthusiasm and urgency get the fire burning, but both can quickly go cold if the wood gives out through delays.

Pulling the Trigger. Understand that for the pro and the amateur alike, the hardest part of most projects is the first step.

Final Note. All that said, projects are a strange animal, predictably unpredictable. Short-term projects were the ones I usually got done. Even for big expeditions, organizers might spend years raising money, getting permits, and building a team, while performers are busy with other projects. Long-term projects are mostly the pleasure of weekend warriors. Experts might need a tune-up period, but it's unlikely they need to learn new skills, only exercise them to the fullest. What's more, an expert's goals evolve, so projects are chosen per their immediate relevance to where the expert is, making short- to medium-term projects more attractive.

Focus and enthusiasm can only be anchored in a project over the short term, lest the expert finds something else to do, since *doing*, not planning, is the expert's prerogative. An expert is more likely to have long-term goals and short-term projects. As celebrated climber and BASE jumper Steph Davis once said, "Things don't stay the same long enough to make long-term plans."

For the rest of us, projects are dreams that we strive to grow into, the stars that we wish upon.

THE 24-HOUR CHALLENGE

Years ago, fitness guru, climber, and biker Steve Edwards (who birthed the popular P90X training programs) started the Birthday Challenge, where people perform a series of feats corresponding to their age. Once the Challenge caught on (website, etc.), people tried to outdo each other with the novelty of their feats. Someone celebrating their 40th birthday might cycle 40 miles, swim 40 laps, drink a 40-ounce beer, play 40 songs with a garage band, and so forth.

Then a twenty-four-year-old Malibu surfer hiked into the hills above Malibu State Park and spent twenty-four hours all alone. The surfer apparently had a boundary experience, like Jesus' in Gethsemane, and persuaded his immediate friends to repeat the adventure. Most early takers did so as a macho dare, figuring if they could surf Trestles in a storm or cycle over Tioga Pass, they could relax for a day, all alone, no problem. Most returned saying, in so many words: "I had no idea." As word got out, the 24-Hour Challenge became a stand-alone event. Time did the rest.

Much as water and dust create an infinite variety of snow-flakes, silence, stillness, and The Remote craft different experiences for all people. There are no instructions for the 24-Hour Challenge because no one can know how the encounter should go. Efforts to direct it only limit your range, but several points are worth knowing going in, conditions that help eliminate hitches that might end the challenge early. Most of these concern safety. Once you are confident that you won't get hurt, the mind is free to drift.

Don't pull the trigger on a full day alone in the wilds till you work out the physical details. This is a stepped process for all but seasoned outdoors people. Determine what kind of terrain and environment feels most natural. You won't find a desert in the Everglades or a delta in Georgia, though many areas feature varied terrain, providing options. Once you find your target area, start extending your solo trips. The aim is not to get miles from nowhere (though that is an option). You want some place where you can spend an entire day in total isolation, where sight and sound of the civilized world is entirely absent.

The easiest option is found in big open spaces, like the high desert in Southern California. You can usually find a random, iso-lated draw or pile of rocks a mile off the road where the chance of someone else going at exactly the same time is virtually zero. Start searching out such places, extending your time there, in total isola-tion, doing nothing. Try it on for size.

For many, the fear is getting attacked by animals, though the chances are *extremely* remote, even in bear country. Another concern is getting lost. A final concern is security, especially for girls and women. No solution fits all areas, but common sense and experience in a given locale will furnish the answers. Much is learned through trial runs. At some point you'll have to commit. Here are a few suggestions.

Pick a target date, preferably when the weather is typically good. Check the weather report to ensure you have a window. You must be able to get in and out of the target site no matter the conditions. Keep your bivouac (overnight) gear basic. Take just enough clothes to keep warm and, if you can stand it, no tent, just a pad and sleeping bag. Avoid stoves and never build a fire. These can disclose your location and distract you from encountering the ancient aloneness, which is the wormhole *in*.

Bring more water than you need but just enough perishable food to sustain you. No booze or drugs. Avoid all extras, especially notepads. Have a phone but only use it for emergencies (though I've never heard of one happening on a well-planned 24-Hour Challenge). Always avoid scrambling or technical terrain where an accident might happen. A buddy system is preferred, where at least one other person, who knows exactly where you are, drops you off and retrieves you at a given time.

Your preparation will provide a taste, but everyone's 24-Hour Challenge is unique. The external world is unlikely to change; the intensity of inner experience, however, is something few foresee. What does this mean? What happens in that place of stillness, which John Muir called "at once awful and sublime"? The 24-Hour Challenge is designed to directly answer that question.

A popular strategy, followed by many, is to never say a word to anyone about your twenty-four hours spent alone. Especially that you did so. You go this one alone. It might be the one thing you'll ever have that is entirely yours.

IMPOSSIBLE MOMENTS

In 1923, during a publicity tour for his trip to the Himalaya, a *New York Times* reporter asked British mountaineer George Mallory why he wanted to climb Mount Everest, the world's highest mountain, and he famously replied, "Because it's there." For going on a century, this spontaneous reply has echoed through Western culture and is commonly trotted out whenever someone tries to justify an unjustifiable objective. Why shoot for the moon? Why explore the depths of the ocean? People die doing that stuff. Because Mallory's answer is indirect, "Because it's there" sounds more like a paradox than an explanation, but the gist seems simple as pie once we understand motivations.

We are programmed to seek comfort and security. But if this is our only metric for living, we eventually rust from the middle. Few have feared this so keenly as George Mallory. "Because it's there" was Mallory's affirmation that if embracing toil and risk were the price for escaping existential corrosion and experiencing magnitude, he would gladly take them. Note that we never ask *why?* of the person going to a NASCAR race or a bull's-only rodeo. Thrill and excitement, if only through proxy, are the straws that stir our drinks. The question always is: How strong a drink do we want or need?

The few Mallorys among us require the 100-proof stuff, stiff doses of enormity, gravity, and the challenges of risk management. But the pull toward comfort and security is never overcome, only momentarily escaped. That's why "Because it's there" is a paradox, a statement that contradicts itself. Not as a trope, but in an *impossible moment*, when our need to escape smallness and boredom crash into suffering, fear, and sometimes death. In 1924, Mallory and his partner, Andrew "Sandy" Irvine, found their impossible moment on the northeast ridge of Everest, while attempting to make the first ascent (on May 1, 1999, my friend Conrad Anker discovered Mallory's frozen corpse on the northern slopes of Everest).

Experienced hands are seasoned through their struggles with impossible moments. No expert mountain biker has not crashed so hard they wished the wheel had never been invented. No long-distance thru-hiker, humping a spine-bending pack up a slushy draw in a hailstorm, has not asked herself a thousand times: What was I *thinking?* When first encountered, impossible moments are violently disorienting because our secret sauce has suddenly gone toxic. For the moment, there's no elixir and no escape. Those first few encounters can be soul crushers, and have ended many promising careers.

Like the time when we were attempting the first coast-to-coast traverse of Borneo, the fifth-largest island on the planet. Our team included climber Jim Bridwell, whitewater guides Jim Slade and Stan Boor, adventure cameraman Peter Pilafian, and alpinist and expedition organizer Rick Ridgeway, who'd come to this equatorial hellhole straight from Mount Everest and looked like a wrung dishrag (he later got typhoid and nearly perished). We were somewhere near the central divide, though nothing was certain. Back then, in 1986, satellite images of the island were unavailable, and the map we had was totally blank in the middle.

With any luck, once we finished trundling down a steep, muddy footpath under triple canopy jungle, we'd find the river and could raft toward the central divide, as the nomadic Punan Dyaks had promised. We had a dozen of them along with us, including the chief, to show the way and help carry loads. After a sixteen-day march from the headwaters of the Kapus, the Punan were just as jungle weary and beat down as we were.

We weren't lucky. When we got to the bottom of the jungled mountainside there was no river, as all had hoped and prayed for. Only a tiny, diamond clear creek, purling in deep shade. The cool water tasted like God after our brutal march but I didn't care. We'd have to slog up and over and all the way down *another* range, and maybe then we'd find the river. The chief hadn't made this march in ten years so he wasn't sure. I was starting to lose it. I stared at the little creek, glanced at Bridwell and said, "Why couldn't this be a river?" Bridwell just looked at me.

We paused and ate lunch, passing around a palm frond full of mushy white rice flecked with jungle *chicharrones*—boiled pig fat stripped off the flank of a wild boar that, two days before, a tribesman had chased down and killed with a machete. The rice tasted like flavorless gruel and the pig fat, shoe leather. Bridwell took a few bits and said, "Why couldn't this taste like pizza pie?" I glared at him, and he said, "Because it ain't." If George Mallory would have stumbled up just then I would have shot him.

We started up the next mountain, the tiny, seldom-used path teeming with leeches, clouds of mosquitoes, and thorny creepers, the jungle cacophony so loud and shrill we had to yell to hear each other. Three hours later we were still trudging uphill, our tongues hanging out because we'd misjudged the height of the range and hadn't brought enough water. By the time we crested the ridge we were all so cooked and dehydrated we panted in reedy gasps. Halfway down the far side, the sky cut loose and drilled the canopy like grapeshot, muddy rivulets streaming down on both sides. I put my lips to the mud and slurped, I was *that* thirsty—and spit out a mouthful of sludge. The jungle, it seemed, was laughing at me.

I started seeing double as we hunkered between the flutes of towering banyans, prey to every mantis and bloodsucker, as lightning dashed the jungle. All I wanted was to be back at that cool shady creek with the water that tasted like God. There was nothing to do but wait, for another two hours, an impossible two hours for sure.

My life, and every life I've ever seen, is nourished by impossible moments, just as new trees live off the deadfall. As every passing year feels increasingly miraculous and impossible, I sometimes wonder why I once sought out what I now have in spades, as I vault toward a moment that really is impossible, a drop with no bottom. "Because it's there," no one gets around the Big Drop; nobody escapes to comfort and security. Perhaps all those times battling the wild places, and myself—across the polar ice cap, on the lone and level sands of the desert, and somewhere in Borneo— were so much practice for my last impossible moment. On the other hand, maybe I just didn't want to get a regular job.

HAUNTED HOUSE

Big Rock was a small, longtime practice climbing area in Southern California, set in a brush-covered hilltop and frequented by the Sierra Club and the Riverside Mountain Rescue Team. Legend has it that Big Rock saw its first activity in the late 1940s, when soldiers from nearby March Air Force Base sieged the water-trough running up the middle of the 150-foot-high face. In the ensuing years, several generations of Los Angeles and San Diego-based climbers filled the gaps, clambering over every square inch of the smooth diorite slab. When we finally showed up, the innovative work had been done. The place was largely abandoned and felt like a lost wing of the Smithsonian, the forty-something routes so many relics of the pioneers who used Big Rock as a testing ground for evolving face climbing techniques.

We were still in high school, anxious to follow the chalk marks of the caste of knights who had dominated Southern California climbing for over a decade—knights who had largely and suddenly vanished. We'd heard all about these guys and yet rarely saw or had met one. Naturally they became mythical figures in our young minds.

Their numbers included Paul and Phil Gleason, Pat Callis, and Charlie Raymond, who developed Suicide Rock when both were grad students at CalTech, the preternatural Phil Haney, Keith Leaman, John Gosling, the ebullient, chain-smoking Don O'Kelly, and a few others (many were members of an ambitious Eagle Scout group, we later learned). On the gritty Big Rock slabs this gang had established a score of difficult climbs, right up to the modern grade. Then they moved on and apparently never returned or looked back. Where were they now? What had gone on here?

Problem was, by the time my generation started climbing, the public was locked out of Big Rock while county workers built the Perris Lake Recreation Area. That never stopped us. We'd park out on the road and sneak in. We were well out of the way of the derricks and skip loaders so by the time a foreman was bothered to chase us off, we usually had scaled a handful of routes and were good to go. When the same cranky boss kept catching us, we worked out an arrangement of leaving a half pint of Old Forester on the boulder near the base of the slab. Then we were free to climb all day—no questions asked. These were simpler times. Once the dam was completed they once again opened Big Rock to climbing, and for the last thirty-five years several generations of So Cal climbers have learned the ropes there.

Our glory days out at Big Rock were when we first visited the place and seemed to have it all to ourselves, knowing we were using the footholds of the climbers who had later established the spectacular climbs up at Suicide and Tahquitz Rocks, where we came of age as adults and as climbers. We knew almost nothing of these shadow figures, but we came to know their handiwork. Their names were lavishly strewn across guidebook pages of all the local venues, but they were gone now and there was nothing but rusty quarter-inch Rawl Drive contraction bolts, widely spaced, to suggest that here at Big Rock they had smoked their Marlboros and told lies and took huge skidding falls, if the rumors are true, taking pictures of each other with Keith Leaman's Kodak Brownie stuffed in a gym sock inside a Folgers Coffee can as they mastered small hold and friction climbing and learned how to engineer face climbs. Back in the day.

Big Rock was but a brief aside of the larger drama we all eventually found in Yosemite and beyond. Its charms are mostly lost on outsiders but were dear to us owing to its regional legacy, which reads like the college diary of the home team. One's early history always exerts a special hold on us; and to every successive generation, Big Rock will feel like a wall of phantoms, when the past meets the present where the rubber meets the rock. It's an unremarkable place but it still feels enchanted, as for a moment in time we had it to ourselves, when the dam was forming up and the entrance fee was a short dog of cheap bourbon.

At an old abandoned crag, the anxious silence reaches back to the long lost who worked out a way before them on the rock. Decades later, at the juncture of back then and not yet, we rope up for a route and climb it right now. Riding old routes into the future. Following the line of phantoms whose bones might well be dust. We are the same ghosts following the same holds, made real at the short span between our fingertips and a razor edge. We dangle side by side at the belay, paying out the memories. The collected astonishment, ingrained in the rock, murmurs to those still on their way. Every route is an enchantment. Every crag is a haunted house.

SAND

While in Del Rio, Texas, covering the legendary Bull's Only Rodeo—an adventure sport if ever there was one—I asked then-world champion all-around rodeo cowboy, Ty Murray, if there was any unspoken code they tried to follow. "No explaining and no complaining," said Ty. "You either get out there and do it, or you don't. Nothing else matters."

If you've ever been around rodeos, you often see celebrations after great rides (like football players dancing in the end zone), which underscore the catharsis we all seek through dramatic encounters, but once the hat is tossed and the cheers die off, the cowboy or cowgirl (barrel racing is every bit of an adventure sport) is typically the picture of modesty, with few words spoken. Here is the self-contained grit cowboys and cowgirls so prize, known in the days of the roundup as "sand." This sand, which trickles through the veins of many people of gravity, is standard tackle on the rodeo circuit, where young broncs and cowgirls, along with the bulk of journeymen players, mortgage life, limb, and every comfort if only to stay in the game.

Only top riders can afford to fly to rodeos, which during the season average several a week in cities sometimes thousands of miles apart. World-class riders often own planes, sometimes hitting two rodeos in the same day, picking and choosing high-profile contests with full purses. Most riders live closer to the bone, forming partnerships with other aspiring pros, following the circuit in rusty old pickups. Win or lose, it's right back into the truck for another all-nighter to another rodeo in Tuscaloosa or Dodge or Tuba City.

If their vehicle doesn't break down, they arrive soon enough to eat and rest, and maybe get a bum elbow rubbed down and taped up as they psych to do battle. Often the journeyman rider wheels in road-warped, hungry and sore, with little or no warm-up, and jumps straight onto a bucking horse or a bull. They'll hang around if they make it through the first go-around, maybe one out of three or four outings. Otherwise it's down the road in the old pickup, all passed out as the sober one drives, chasing a dream wherever the stock is bucking. It's a tough go, but they aren't asking for sympathy and they won't get any.

The all-night rides in beater trucks, the throbbing limbs, crappy meals, and gloomy defeats—these put the *sand* in an adventurer's veins. We find it in all adventure sports, from soul surfers to the weekend warriors gathered below every sport crag from Australia to Hong Kong. They hold the tattered flag of the old idealized archetype, who stay the course with a few bucks in their pocket and a love for the game and the people involved. Social media gives everyone their moments in the sun, but what we all seek in the wild places is direct and meaningful experience, not a cyber facsimile, and not something that is merely fun

As the man said, "You either get out there and do it, or you don't. Nothing else matters."

HOMECOMING

I first went to Yosemite Valley as a wannabe rock star when I was seventeen years old, and continued to spend every summer there until I was twenty-five. Like most climbers, I stayed in Camp 4 (now on the National Register of Historic Places), which back then was girded on the east end by the Camp 4 parking lot, an oily acre crammed with the proudest medley of rust buckets imaginable, including an ancient British step van that must have been parked on the street during the blitzkrieg; a dented, salt-pocked Cadillac, now a convertible thanks to a cutting torch; and a red VW van, broadsided, t-boned, rear-ended, and rolled, not a window in it, vise grips where the steering wheel should have been. Few of these ran without priming and a push start. There wasn't a treaded tire in the whole lot, and a live battery got passed back and forth like a gold brick. The license plates were from Canada, Washington, California, Colorado—most of these junkers having been babied down the road with little chance of ever reaching the valley, and no chance of ever leaving it.

Beyond the parking lot lay dozens of colorful tents pitched in a swath of wooded shade. In the summertime, between two cinderblock bathrooms at both ends of camp, many of the world's best rock climbers called this place home. Other legitimate campgrounds, full of tourists, RVs, and screaming kids, featured kiosks full of rangers, who were full of silly rules, but during the first few summers I spent in Camp 4, I rarely saw a ranger. The park service had essentially roped the place off, much as Hawaii, back when leprosy swept through the Pacific, had quarantined the island of Moloka'i. With no rangers and no regulations, and in the almost complete absence of women, the place was basically an international flophouse.

In the ensuing decades, women joined the party, harmonizing and inspiring the adventure world, which had largely remained a boy's club, but the human tendency for like-minded folks, of all makes and models, to assemble around a classic venue in pursuit of a shared activity, has been around for ages. Every winter, surfers gather on the North Shore of Oahu, Hawaii, to ride the huge waves at Waimea Bay, Pipeline, Sunset Beach, and other local breaks. During summer in Europe, BASE jumpers pour into Lauerbrunnen, Switzerland, to launch off dozens of sheer peaks and crave the sky in wingsuits. The list of sites is as long as the games we play, and the reasons are just as many, but at bottom, we need only look to human nature to get a bead on motivations.

Young people run on passion, and when we peel back the particulars we find the timeless need to love something. Without that love, life is a slog. Then we die. We are a species sustained by desires, and the young among us can make no sense of life without a target for their dreams. When we find it, in an activity and, in turn, in a venue where all hearts beat as one, we experience a homecoming. We find our place, and that sense of belonging makes the world go round despite the inevitable grief and fallout.

The outdoor arena has always served as an area for passionate people to do something, and as a place for others to go and to be. In both cases The Remote holds out the promise of belonging to something bigger than ourselves and the cans dragging noisily behind us. The landscape of this homecoming is big as the Sahara, a theme we'll mine through the adventure of these pages.

For those who feel this is overstated, consider this: If you were to ask fifty people for whom the outdoors has become their haven, half if not more of them would promise that hiking, biking, climbing, or (fill in the blank) had literally saved them. That's a power. That's a milieu that potentially is greater than our problems, our conditioning, and our pasts. For some, myself included, that power was more than a homecoming. It was deliverance.

People

THE RABBI

Most of my classes were killing me so I welcomed the rare fluff course that offered full credit. So did everyone else, so it wasn't till the start of my sophomore year that I got a chair in The Rabbi's *Birding in the Greater Pomona Valley*, the alluvial basin formed by the Santa Ana River and its tributaries, where my little college was situated.

Mort Novak was no rabbi, but everyone called him that because he always wore a yarmulke and looked hard into things. At the start of the first class someone asked why there was no textbook and The Rabbi read a passage by T. S. Elliot warning never to read commentary about a poem till you read the poem itself, neat, like sight-reading sheet music. This was The Rabbi's third time teaching the bird watching course, and the way things had gone, students didn't watch birds so much as they watched the birding guide. Elliot wouldn't like that, and The Rabbi hated it. So this class would learn ornithology through direct observation. "Then we'll write our own book," said The Rabbi. Here was a man working out a problem. Now we were part of it.

Each of us fifteen students were issued a pair of high-powered binoculars, then we followed The Rabbi out to the leafy courtyard in the Humanities Center and started scanning the big sycamore trees for birds. It wasn't till I had a woodpecker in the cross-hairs that I realized I had never *seen* a bird except for crows on powerlines or the toucans in the zoo. Of course birds were every-where in Southern California, or anywhere there is water (there currently are around fifty birds per person on earth), but I noticed them only in passing, and never in such handsome detail. Still, the book proposal felt unlikely. The class was full of science geeks, wannabe novelists, and fussy, brainiac girls who could recite *The Bell Jar* from memory—hardly the squad to beat the bush looking for vultures.

"You'll need to keep notes," said The Rabbi, as he handed out Champion Wiremaster 100-sheet notebooks (still have mine). "And keep the binos with you." That was it. Students squirmed. Barely an hour into *Birding*, and the course and The Rabbi were feeling monolithic. Who didn't avail themselves of available data when writing about any phenomenon? one egghead wanted to know. The Rabbi didn't care. Whatever Darwin did down in the Galápagos, do that.

The unknown is daunting. Even if it's just looking at birds in the sky whose Latin names you can't yet state or pronounce. How do I know what I'm looking at? What if my descriptions are all wrong? The plus side is that as a total ignoramus, I enjoyed a near vertical learning curve, so long as I paid attention. It also made me curious.

Walking across campus for whatever reason, I found myself noticing the ubiquitous sound of birds, stopping to glass a robin or a jay, sometimes earning style points with the ladies, which to some's chagrin is an ongoing concern for male coeds. I lived in the dorms, in an upstairs room the size of a broom closet, made bear-able by throwing open the window, giving view to a big Fremont's cottonwood where birds of many feathers gathered as I skimmed excruciating passages from James Fenimore Cooper. Who was piping that melody, that two-note screech, that funky warbling, background sounds, long ignored, that clarified once I matched a refrain to a particular bird. That was the start of it. My Wiremaster started filling out.

Of course, comparing notes with other students was a shit show without some point of reference. The only birds we could recognize by name were doves, sparrows, crows, woodpeckers, and hawks, which arrived in such variety we never were sure if Sheila's description fit the same bird Josh was talking about. Good point, said The Rabbi, who dragooned the photographer for the school newspaper, also a student in our class, who spent several days photographing the birds roosting in the sycamores nearby (and he later went far afield). The inside of the Rabbi's classroom soon resembled the aviary wing of the Audubon Society, with 8x10 photos of birds covering the walls. That's when the course caught fire, when we could start matching notes in our Wiremasters with a photo on the wall.

Names were needed in this regard, and The Rabbi said to come up with our own, so we did: Orange Dinky (house finch); Cue Ball (California towhee); Sky Jacket (scrub jay); Candy Ass (yellow-rumped warbler); Pibald (black phoebe); Siren (song sparrow), et al.

To get anywhere with our book project, we couldn't all be watching the same species, said The Rabbi. We had to pick one bird to follow and document. I went with the Windjammer (red-tailed hawk). I'd spotted one on our first field trip to nearby Puddingstone Reservoir. So did LeRoy, from Compton, California, who looked like Eldridge Clever but could crunch numbers with Euclid. At the Rabbi's suggestion, LeRoy and I teamed up to chase down some hawks. Other students joined forces in search of Cue Balls and Sky Jackets. The Rabbi provided no information beyond where a party might find a given bird. Flight patterns, eating habits, family life—this and whatever else we found was the meat and feathers of our future book.

After several months of information gathering, The Rabbi handed out several bird books and we started comparing data, much of which we already knew by heart, having learned it first-hand. Of course this method is impractical for those on a tight schedule, who benefit from research and planning before most any trip or excursion. Point is, objective data was first gleaned from direct observation, and the more that we can source through immediate experience, the richer the life we lead. When we know what we're looking for, the experience is not the same as when we encounter something sight unseen, before names and labels.

Experiencing something with fresh eyes and no preconceptions is the thrill of discovery. This was the idea when Dumas said to go to Paris and get lost, that you'd never forget it that way. Even now, thirty-five years after my semester with The Rabbi, I still scan the sky and the treetops for Orange Dinkys and Sky Jackets. When I see one, it's a wonderful thing.

EL TIBURON

This all happened on Margarita Island, before Venezuela became a failed state in the early 2000s, when water sports were huge and Christmastime brought thousands of tourists escaping grim European winters.

During an afternoon jog down by Playa Varadero, my cousin Carlitos and I noticed a crew erecting bleachers on the sand and inflating an arch that would serve as the finish and starting line for an open ocean swimming race. Triathletes and watermen were arriving from all over to compete. An Olympic hopeful from the national team was favored to win, but local money was on a Cuban named Rubio. A big motor launch had dropped anchor a mile and a half offshore—the turnaround point for the out-and-back swim—and a tethered blimp was hovering above it.

According to an organizer, a local fisherman named El Tiburon was scheduled to perform a short demonstration swim before the official race kicked off. I'd heard a little about El Tiburon (shark, in Spanish), mostly from old fishermen who drank too much. In the days before motors, El Tiburon was said to have swum the nets out with a rope lashed round his waist, sometimes getting separated from the flotilla and having to swim ashore from way out. He was a legend, though his name was heard less and less these days because he was going on eighty. The man was real but the stories, we figured, were not. The next day, Carlitos and I showed up for the race. So, it seemed, did half the people on the island.

An athlete's-only area near the start quickly filled with swimmers small-talking and psyching each other up. The competitors included several female athletes as well, including a Mexican named Prima Doña, an alabaster giantess with close-cropped, bleach-blonde hair. Rubio, the Cuban favorite, resembled a deep-fried James Dean. Even had the pout. With all this going on we hardly noticed the old man pushing a bike across the sand.

"That's gotta be him," said Carlitos.

El Tiburon was taller than I had imagined, around 6 feet, more golden than brown, with barnyard shoulders and a saint's face as rucked and seamed as the floor of Lago Maracaibo. He set his bike against a railing, padlocked it, then walked over to a spray unit set up to cool the racers, where he stood in the misty curtain like a triton in a fountain, staring out to sea.

Never mind any demonstration swim, El Tiburon had come there to race, something so incidental to the proper competition it got only casual mention over the loudspeaker. We stood outside the roped-off area and had a clear view of the other athletes, who hardly noticed and didn't care about the wrinkled old fisherman swimming in their race.

"Cuatro, tres, dos, uno—"

The gun sounded and the swimmers stormed across the sand and dove into the sea, surfacing in a flurry, their arms thrashing the water. All but El Tiburon, who walked toward the water on unsteady legs. The main pack was well out in front when El Tiburon duck-dove under the shore break and took his first stroke, which brought a charity roar from the crowd. Carlitos and I climbed up to a bluff overlook, where we could see the race unfold.

The pack quickly lengthened into a loose chain, churning past small breakers in the shallows and clearing a sea ledge where the ocean floor dropped off and the water went from gray to Persian blue. In open ocean at last, swirling currents yanked the chain apart, sending the pack in all directions, like a stain spreading out on a blue tablecloth. An onshore wind and low rolling swells doubled their trouble. A swimmer was lucky to pull a couple clean strokes before getting hauled sideways by the rip. The stronger swimmers held a ragged trajectory, but they were covering 15 or 20 feet to gain 10 on the motor launch and the turnaround, still better than a mile out to sea.

Far behind, El Tiburon swam at a casual but fluid clip. Once he pulled into open water he was little affected by the violent riptides, and seemed to glide through hidden troughs, now hitchhiking onto the offshore edge of whorls that thrust him out at speed, as if he and the currents were on speaking terms. Slowly he closed the distance with the stragglers in the main pack.

"Old fart might make that boat out there," said Carlitos.

We watched the swimmers shrink to specks, then occasional white flashes. Then only a working sea stretched vacantly out to the motor launch and the tethered blimp, two dots bobbing on the blue horizon. It'd take a while for the swimmers to stroke back into view, so we headed over to the hot dog cart and went to work alongside hundreds of others jammed on the bluff. A buzz from the mob let us know that the swimmers were returning.

"Holy shit," said Carlitos, who'd begged a set of binoculars off a Dutch tourist and was glassing the open ocean. The swimmers were growing on the horizon, and we moved in a crush over to the edge of the bluff. Carlitos handed me the binos and I framed up the first three swimmers, roughly moving together, several hundred yards in front of the others. El Tiburon was one of them.

The Dutch tourist snatched back his binos, and Carlitos and I scrambled down to the beach. Word quickly spread and "El Tiburon" was repeated a thousand times in thirty seconds. According to the man screaming over the loudspeaker, we were witnessing a miracle.

El Tiburon was not so much swimming as navigating the rips and whorls. Now the other two, Rubio the Cuban and Prima Doña, were trying to track the old man's course, but lacking his feel for the currents, they could only compensate with furious strokes. Slowly they tired and fell back as El Tiburon, with the wind and swells behind him, squirted over the sea ledge, snagged a gentle comber, and bodysurfed up onto the sand.

What we'd seen that day was a demonstration in efficiency, a crucial factor in every outdoor activity. Technique and equipment are "good" when they are efficient. That is, we can clean the floor with a Q-tip, but a mop and a bucket are better because they are more efficient. El Tiburon could never keep pace with the other two in an Olympic pool, but out there in open ocean, on this squirrelly watered, windward side of the island, El Tiburon was nonpareil.

GRAB YOUR STUFF

During my late teens I spent most spring weekends at Tahquitz and Suicide Rocks, in the mountains above Palm Springs, usually with hometown partners Richard Harrison and Rick Accomazzo, who later became trendsetters in American climbing. We converged on these local crags as a warm-up for Yosemite, then points beyond, so the aim was to log mileage on the rock, to get ready for the big stuff in May.

By late afternoon we normally had bagged the day's projects, so we'd kick back at a clearing below the Weeping Wall, Suicide's traditional hangout and pack dump, surrounded by other stragglers and die-hards. No one had decided on how best to close out the day. Somewhere during these idle moments, always fretful with kids on fire, Richard started asking around if anyone had some route they dreamed of doing, but had never tried or done.

The bulk of this crew were older, recreational climbers, not die-hards like us, so odds were we'd already ticked their dream route.

Most had one climb in particular that they could only imagine ever doing, to which all other routes were measured, but was too impossible to mention. Richard's knack was getting total strangers to imagine out loud.

Richard never gave them time to consider failure, or to start confessing how they had no business ... cha cha cha. The moment Ted from Alhambra or Roxy from New Paltz mentioned a route name, Richard grabbed his pack and said, "Grab your stuff, we're going there now."

Richard wasn't going without us. So Rick and I enlisted the nearest bodies and in half an hour we had a regular conga line charging up the rock. Much of the fun derived from the improbability of the adventure. We never would have led groups for the Sierra Club or any of the other outfits who frequented the rocks back then, futzing around with boring safety drills while many, we reckoned, dreamed of just climbing, as we did. Some, we had seen, were highly skilled, but were handcuffed by group responsibilities and protocols. It was like watching tigers mill in a cage at the zoo. Richard felt this, yanked open the door, and a hundred dreams were instantly rekindled. The tigers hadn't died, but it felt like a resurrection to see them roaring for the first time in years as they showed their teeth, scratched, and fought Old Man Gravity on his own terms. "Mass assault" is what we called it, and we never had such fun, yelling at the top of our lungs, "coaching" people, some sixty years old, up stuff they never thought they would climb in 1,000 lifetimes. For some, what felt like larks were crowning achievements, and charmed because they were shared.

They held a memorial for Richard down in Blue Diamond, Nevada, just south of his beloved Red Rocks, after his untimely death a few years ago. The many professionals he had partnered with sent condolences, and a few of them showed up, but most of the crowd were those who ten or thirty years before had heard the words they'd never forget: "Grab your stuff, we're going there now."

FOREST THERAPY GUIDES

My good friend Charlotte started as a river guide when she was seventeen, then taught backcountry skiing for twenty years and, during summer months, ran wilderness training courses for Special Forces, and throughout was an avid peak bagger, trail runner, and sky diver. She was, as they say, *The Shit*.

Instructors from the Forest Therapy movement had gotten hold of her in the hopes of expanding their curriculum. Charlotte was nothing if not thorough, and before making any recommendations, she went through the certification process herself, to learn what the program was about. Then she organized a one-day retreat in the pine forests around Idyllwild, the mile-high hamlet in the mountains above Palm Springs, in Southern California, ground zero for rednecks, aging movie stars, rock musicians fresh out of rehab, wealthy weekenders, and the budding New Age movement, with its heavenly creeds and flavorless food. I'd grown up climbing on Tahquitz and Suicide Rocks, just above Idyllwild, and knew the area well, so Charlotte invited me along to assist on her retreat, explaining the basics about Forest Therapy on the drive up.

We met a dozen Forest Therapy instructors at a vegan (of course) restaurant in Idyllwild and carpooled up to the turnout. As it happens during commercial retreats, a Forest Therapy Guide facilitates gentle, risk-free walks, providing instructions ("invitations") for "sensory opening activities" along the way. These walks follow a standard sequence, beginning with centering exercises to encourage "conscious embodied contact" with the present moment and place. Next come a series of connective invitations, often improvised on the spot and adapted to client needs. These are followed by wander time, or simply sitting in one place.

An entire walk lasts two to four hours and rarely covers more than a quarter mile. In that short distance most clients (which numbered few familiar with the outdoors) experience a deeper connection with nature and encounter a wide range of experiences, some significant, even profound.

During Charlotte's retreat, she ran the dozen or so present through the very same course that she was taught, and at the end asked them what they thought. Initially, most were confused, and when pressed, admitted they were disappointed that she had brought nothing new to the group. What might "something new" look like, Charlotte asked, going around the group and giving each instructor one minute to blurt out their immediate impressions, before they had time to think about it.

Inside of fifteen minutes the instructors had a slew of suggestions on how to tweak their program to achieve greater effect, which carried greater import because it came from the instructors themselves, derived from their direct experience.

As is so often the case, the only thing required to revamp the curriculum was a shift in the guide's perspective. Since Nature is second to none in this regard, and the instructors already had proven methods, once they applied them to themselves, not as a "witness" but as participants, the way ahead was clear, but it took a coach of Charlotte's skill to ever pull this off.

FREJA

Diego was a tour guide who took tourists on simple nature hikes on the island of Margarita, down in Venezuela. He worked for Hilton Hotels, and his morning strolls along the beach and through nearby jungle were favorites among wealthy Europeans, who flew over in droves during Christmas break, when in Stockholm and Zurich the snow was barn high and the *föhn* wind howled. One morning I shagged along when he took a group of Danish tourists on walkabout.

The Danes numbered a dozen or so, none younger than fifty, were respectful to a fault, civil but chilly, and asked more questions than an eight-year-old. Except Freja. She didn't say a word. Like the others, she was overdressed for the sweltering tropics, in her crepe silk slacks and linen blouse. Her graying blond hair was torqued into a glossy bun the size of an acorn. Her carriage was painfully regal, her face attractive but blank, and she didn't so much walk as march, stiffly, across the beach sand and into the leafy jungle, as though attending a coronation. Or a funeral. The others kept asking Diego about the narrow footpath, the spiraling vines, the squawking birds, though I'm guessing since they kept switching between English and German. Diego's father was British and he'd gone to school in Berlin, and the Danes, who treasure education, were impressed with his language skills.

A quarter mile into the jungle we found a wide, flat clearing floored with spongy turf, like an overgrown putting green. The Danes stamped curiously on the turf, then went in twos to a bubbling spring close by. Except Freja, apparently single, who stood like a statue on the edge of the grass.

Diego, besides being a card shark and reggaeton drummer, had a knack for discovering what people were up against, and right on the spot, could reckon a way to escape it. Virtually all of his clients were one-and-done, people unlikely to ever take another tour or to experience jungle again, so he only had one shot of leaving them with something valuable, which greatly distilled his instruction.

I was rummaging in my pack for water when I saw Diego coax a few words out of Freja. She relaxed a notch after a few exchanges, and when Diego asked her an apparently probing question, she smirked and glanced at me (I don't speak a word of German and couldn't follow their drift). I smiled; Freja shrugged, kicked off her shoes, and slowly walked out across the spongy turf, tentatively at first, her toes probing the green stuff. Diego said to keep walking (I think), and with each step I watched the brittle tension drain from her body, till she paused in the middle, and with her arms slightly outstretched and her palms turned up, she smiled up at the sky as she turned in a slow 360.

The others returned from the spring. Freja slipped her shoes back on, and as Diego led the group back to the pool at the Hilton, Freja's face once again went blank as she slipped back into her regal carriage.

Later, answering my question, Diego said he asked Freja how she'd walk if nobody was watching. She'd glanced at me because I *was* watching, but the question was too inviting, so she shrugged, kicked off her shoes, and broke out into the open. Of course we never saw her again, and I imagine she went back to Aalborg or Odense, taut, blank, and majestic, as she'd arrived in Margarita. But she'd always have that moment on the green turf, when Freja from Denmark climbed down off her throne and walked among the living.

OUT-AND-BACKS

The true trail masters are the old-timers found in outing clubs and conservation groups like the Sierra Club, where the institution of day outings is well established and reaches back to the early 1900s. Most outings are organized around a traditional goal, often the top of a peak, a practice that birthed the term, "peak baggers."

During college I had a girlfriend, Janet, whose father, Chuck, was a legend in American rock climbing and a longtime trip leader for the Sierra Club. I was a hard-core rock climber, as was Janet, who additionally was a national champion in several sports, an athletic prodigy for sure. We did so much hiking getting to and from climbs that, for me, devoting a weekend just to hiking seemed lame. Though my outdoor career had started by hiking in the San Gabriel Mountains above my home in Upland, California, once I started in with adventure sports, hiking only made sense if it was to get to some place to climb or (insert adventure here, bike or ski).

Like many caught up in the exploding adventure sports revolution, I considered hikers and peak baggers dusty duffers who could not or would not tackle technical terrain. Scaredy-cats who took to the trails by default. Janet assured me I had no idea. "Those people would ruin you," she said, not as an insult but a dare. I took it.

The following weekend we joined a Sierra Club group making a one-day ascent of Mount Gorgornio, which at 11,503 feet, is the highest peak in Southern California, and a rite of passage for So Cal hikers. I fell in behind a group of about twenty-five, ages thirty to seventy-five, whose dust I ate for the next eight hours. Especially annoying were the breaks we'd take, when I'd collapse back, sucking air, while most of the others scrambled far and wide, checking out the wreckage of old planes that had slammed into the mountain (Frank Sinatra's mother was lost in a plane crash on this mountain), say, or climbing a far ridge to get a better photo. I was among the last stragglers to stumble onto the summit of "Old Grayback," a peak I had always neglected for the "real thing."

The lesson learned is that in every corner of the outdoor world there are people who have worked that quadrant into an art form. Even the most mundane-sounding pursuit has a dedicated band of aficionados whose performance, knowledge, and mastery is an endless source of interest and inspiration. And watch out for that seventy-year-old fogey with the knee socks and felt alpine hat. She'll hike you right into the tundra.

TOBIN SORENSON

Tobin Sorenson had the body of a welterweight, a mop of sandy brown hair, and the faraway gaze of the born maniac. He lived with all the innocence of a child, but out on the sharp end of the climbing rope he was Igor unchained. Over the previous summer he'd logged a string of spectacular falls that should have ended his career, and his life, ten times over. Yet he shook each fall off and clawed straight back onto the route for another go, and usually succeeded. He became a world-class climber very quickly because anyone that well-formed and motivated gains the top in no time—if he doesn't kill himself first. One time up at Tahquitz Rock (above the mountain hamlet of Idyllwild, California), while attempting the first free ascent of a route called *Green Arch*, it almost did.

There were four of us: Rick Accomazzo, Richard Harrison, Tobin, and myself. At the base of the *Green Arch*, we studied the steep face leading to the small, vertical corner that soared up for 80 feet before arching right and melding into a field of knobs and pockets. We figured if we could only get to those knobs, the remaining 300 feet would go easily and the *Green Arch* would fall.

Richard and I both took a shot, and I finally reached a rest hold where the arch swept out right and dissolved into that field of knobs. Twenty feet to pay dirt, but those 20 feet looked desperate. There were some big sucker holds just above the arch, but those ran out after about 25 feet and would leave a climber in no-man's land, with nowhere to go, no chance to climb back right onto the route, no chance to get any protection, and no chance to retreat. We'd have to stick to the arch. Finally, I underclung about 10 feet out the arch, whacked in a suspect piton, clipped the rope in—and fell off. I lowered to the ground.

Tobin—who'd suffered through the previous hour circling and doing jumping jacks—tied into the lead rope and stormed up the corner, battled up to the rest hold, drew a few quick breaths, and underclung out to the crappy piton I'd driven straight up into the arch—so bad that I was amazed it held my weight as I lowered back to the ground. Had Tobin traversed right from there, the now-standard free route, he would have gained tall cotton. Instead he just gunned it straight up for glory, cranking himself over the arch and heaving up the line of big sucker holds.

"No!" I screamed up. "Those holds don't go anywhere!"

But it was too late.

Climbing, as it were, with blinders on, Tobin would sometimes claw his way into the most heinous jams. When he'd dead-end, with nowhere to go and looking at a Homeric peeler, the full impact of his folly would hit him like a wrecking ball. He would panic, wail, weep openly, and do perfectly jackass things. Sure enough, about 25 feet above the arch those sucker holds ran out, and Tobin had nowhere to go.

To appreciate Tobin's quandary, understand that he was 25 feet above the last piton, which meant he was looking at a 50-foot fall, since a leader falls twice as far as he is above the last piece of protection. The belayer, tending the other end of the rope, can rarely reel in much rope during a fall because it happens so quickly. Basically, he can only secure the rope—lock it off.

The gravest news was that I knew the piton I'd bashed under the roof could never hold a 50-foot whipper. On gigantic falls, the top piece often rips out, but the fall is broken sufficiently for a lower nut or piton to stop you. Maybe. In Tobin's case, the next lower piece was some dozen feet below the top one, at the rest hold; so in fact, Tobin was looking at close to an 80-footer—plus a few yards more with rope stretch. If he was lucky, the rope would arrest him before he hit the ground—but just barely.

Now as Tobin wobbled far overhead, who should lumber up to our little group but his very father, a Lutheran minister—a sober, retiring, imperturbable gentleman who hacked and huffed from his long march up to the cliff. After hearing so much about climbing from Tobin, he'd finally come to see his son in action. It was like a page from a B-movie script: us cringing and digging in, waiting for the bomb to drop; the good preacher, wheezing through his moustache, sweat-soaked and confused, squinting up at the fruit of his loins; and Tobin, knees knocking, screaming like a woman in labor and looking to plunge off at any second. There is always something you can do, even in the worst situation, if only you keep your nerve. But Tobin was gone, so mastered by terror that he seemed willing to die to be done with it. He glanced down. His face was a study. Suddenly he screamed, "Watch me! I'm gonna jump."

We didn't immediately understand what he meant.

"Jump off?" Richard yelled up.

"Yes!" Tobin wailed.

"NO!" we all screamed in unison.

"You can do it, son!" the preacher put in.

Pop was just trying to put a good face on it, God bless him, but his was the worst possible advice because there was no way Tobin could do it. Or anybody could do it. There were no holds. But inspired by his father's urging, Tobin reached out for those knobs so far to his right, now lunging, now pawing the air as the falling man grabs for a cobweb.

And then he was off.

The top piton shot out and Tobin shot off into the grandest fall I've ever seen a climber take and walk away from, rag-dolling down the wall with dull thuds. But the lower piton held, and he finally jolted onto the rope. For a moment he simply hung there, upside down and moaning. Then Richard lowered him off and he lay motionless on the ground and nobody moved or said a word. You could have heard a pine needle hit the deck. Tobin was peppered with abrasions and had a lump the size of a turnip over one eye. He lay dead still for a moment longer, then wobbled to his feet and shuddered.

"I'll get it next time," he grumbled.

"There ain't gonna be no next time," said Richard.

"Give the boy a chance," the preacher said, thumping Tobin on the back.

When a father can watch his son pitch 80 feet down a vertical cliff and straightaway argue that we were shortchanging the boy by not letting him climb back up and have a second chance at an even longer whistler, we knew the man was cut from the same crazy cloth as Tobin, and that there was no reasoning with him—but the fall had sucked the air out of the whole adventure, and we were through for the day.

Tobin would go on to solo the north face of the Matterhorn and the *Walker Spur* and the *Shroud* on the Grandes Jorasses, would make the first alpine ascent of the *Harlin Direct* on the Eiger, the first ascent of the *Super Couloir* on the Dru, would repeat the hardest free climbs and big walls in Yosemite, and would sink his teeth into the Himalaya. He was, by most estimates, the world's foremost all-around climber during the late 1970s, but he wanted a life full of impossible things no human could ever achieve, so he climbed as if time were too short for him, pumping all the disquietude, anxiety, and nervous waste of a normal year into each route.

I've traveled many miles since those early days at Tahquitz, have done my share of crazy things, and have seen humanity with all the bark on, primal and raw, but I've never since experienced the cosmic rush of watching Tobin, reaching for the promised land. He finally found it in 1980, attempting a solo winter ascent of Mount Alberta's north face. His death was a tragedy, of course.

Yet I've often wondered if God could no longer bear the strain of watching Tobin lunging way out there on the sharp end of the rope, and finally just drew him into the fold.

Another Note about Tobin

Indecision is dangerous when you carry on without fully committing. On the other hand, committing without a plan, simply gassing it pell-mell, is the best way to crash-land. Yet that's what Tobin did, time after time. None of us had ever seen a person charge like Tobin, and straight into hostile fire. As best as I can figure it, Tobin trusted that if he put himself into a position where he had to make it, or die, he would find a way, or the good Lord would for him (Tobin was a born-again Christian).

Golf pro Jack Burke Jr. said that to win a tournament, the Lord had to put his hand on your head. In Tobin's case, judging by his many narrow escapes, the Lord must have grabbed Tobin by the collar and hauled him to safety. There's no logical way to explain or fathom the closeness of his shaves. Even when he rose to greatness and knew the game as well as anyone, Tobin always climbed at a level beyond his capacities, and somehow survived. For a while. But not even the Chosen One can always be so lucky, and going for broke killed him in the end.

None of us ever really got past Tobin's death. He was magical, prodigious—a stone-cold crazy child of a man. We all loved him, but there was nothing at all to learn about his methods, which were so dangerous we need not warn others to avoid them, since they would never occur to any sane person.

The wilds are big enough to accommodate all comers, and to claim a few as their own. That's all the sense I can make out of it.

AVOID IT ALTOGETHER

Ed was an Olympic kayaker whom I met on Idaho's Salmon River back when he taught a five-day symposium to the Junior National Whitewater Team. His students called him *Mister* Ed, after the talking horse on the old TV show, who "never talked . . . unless he had something to say." The Junior Team's assignment was to follow Ed's line through *Split Rock, Salmon Falls, Big Mallard, Elk Bar*, and the other Class III rapids on "The River of No Return," rowdier than normal owing to unusually high spring flow.

The Juniors were skilled and motivated and followed Ed's lead like a pod of dolphins, thrilled to escape running all those boring gates on the Dickerson Whitewater Course, a converted concrete spillway beneath a power plant in Maryland. Because Ed said so little, nobody was sure what they were supposed to be practicing, but the Salmon was a wild river with burly rapids, and that was enough.

On the afternoon of the last day, the flotilla pulled into *Chittam Rapid* with some Juniors screaming out loud as they skirted close to a howling "keeper" hole: a no-exit maw of whitewater that can "keep" anything drawn inside, recirculating everything from driftwood to unfortunate paddlers. They'd followed Ed past dozens of other holes on the Salmon, but nothing like this one.

Soon as they washed into the calm water below *Chittam*, the Juniors pulled over to a sandbar and ran back upstream to stare at the howling cavity, smacking each other's backs and shaking their hands in the air like they were on fire. Quite naturally they wanted to know how to get out of such a hole if they were to get stuck in one.

"Important thing is to avoid the hole altogether," said Ed, "which is what we've been practicing for the last five days."

DRAINS OUT THE BAD

I was on the road in western Kentucky, teaching wilderness skills for a trendy clothing manufacturer, when I met Bilbo, who looked a little like Humphrey Bogart in *High Sierra*. Bilbo had been in and out of jail—mostly in—till he got paroled, at age fifty-two, after doing a "dime" for holding up a convenience store in Pee Wee Valley. Then he found caving, and started working with youth offenders. The arrangement, as I understood it, was that Bilbo was a freelancer, not part of any proper organization. Over the years he'd gained the trust of the authorities, and his short field trips were offered as rewards for good behavior. So it worked well for all involved. Maybe I'd like to join him and see what he was up to?

Next morning I met Bilbo, his two assistants, James and Norman, along with twenty-three young offenders culled from halfway houses and detox centers. Most of the class were raw, restless, scattered, and defiant, and there was no way to otherwise keep them together save that once we were inside the cave there was nowhere else to go but to keep crawling and duckwalking over a mile into a Kentucky catacomb.

By spelunking standards, the cave was unremarkable. No rivers or sinkholes or flowstone sculptures. The first hundred feet of cave was peppered with names spray painted on the walls. We soon dead-ended in a big, sandy-floored cave room, more dungeon than not.

The students were instructed to spread out and lie back in the sand, the beams of their headlamps crisscrossing in the darkness at the ceiling 40 feet overhead, and the bare stone walls.

"Ok," said Bilbo, "on the count of three, everyone turn off your headlamps."

The moment the lights went out murmurs, whispers, and eventually a scream sounded out and someone, followed by everyone else, flipped their headlamps back on. In a deep cave like this one, you couldn't see your hand in front of your face. And you can't hear a thing.

Bilbo kept having the class turn off their headlamps and by that method, eventually culled the class down to three people, a young black girl and two men in their mid-twenties, covered with jailhouse tats. All the others had been led out to the light by James and Norman, who took them on a hike. Bilbo later told me only a few in any group can stand the silence and darkness, and those are the few he could help.

In the few years he'd been guiding addicts and offenders into caves, over fifty people had been "saved" by the silence. Not by itself, of course, but it changed people to the extent that the other modes of recovery could take hold. Perhaps for kids whose history is full of broken glass, the past weighs so heavily on them they can never escape it, but even the darkest past is swallowed by the silence of the void. Most reel. A precious few experience a flash of freedom never imagined. Not much, to be sure, but castles are built on a sliver of hope.

"Somehow, it drains out the bad," said Bilbo, as we drove back to town in his old pickup. At least that's what it done to me. Drop at a time. Don't know how it all works, really. Only that it does—for some."

True story.

No Coming Back

Local mountain guide Fred Husoy, BASE jumping pioneer Carl Boenish, and I shouldered our packs and started up shifty moraines toward a snowy col and the leg-busting trudge for the summit of Norway's Trollveggen Wall, Europe's tallest vertical rock face—a brooding gneiss hulk featuring several notorious rock climbs, and the proposed site of our world-record BASE jump. BASE is the acronym for parachuting from a B: building, A: antenna, S: span (bridge), or E: earth (cliff).

A week earlier, back in Los Angeles, as Carl raked through his garage full of gear, we'd talk—or rather he'd preach—about Baby Jesus, Coco Joe, or whoever. Suddenly Carl would dash to his piano and butcher some Brahms or Brubeck, then jump back into conversation, his drift ranging from electrical engineering to terra-cotta sculpture to trampolines and particle physics, galvanized by a screwy amalgam of mysticism and personal revelations. Often he would heave all this out in the same sprawling rant. One of the other producers working on our show—a biannual CBS special based on the Guinness Book of World's Records—thought Carl was on LSD, but Carl's laugh was so large and his fire so hot I found myself giddy by the inspired way he met the world. Different as we were, both of us were drawn to crazy shit. In the fellowship of adventurers, people like Carl Boenish drove the bus.

Finally we gained the summit ridge, beyond which the wall dropped 6,000 feet to the Trondheim Valley. The clouds parted and we lay belly-down and stuck our heads out over the vast, sucking drop as Carl laid out his requirements. The wall beneath his launch site must overhang for hundreds of feet, he said, long enough for a plunging BASE jumper to reach near-terminal velocity. Only at top speed, when the air became thick as water, could his lay-out positioning create enough horizontal draft to track—actually fly out and away from the wall to pop the chute. A decade later, wingsuits would change all this, but that's how it was in 1982. Back then, state-of-the-art parachutes didn't simply drop vertically, but sported a three-to-one glide ratio—3 feet forward for every 1 foot down. It was not unheard of for twisted lines to deploy a chute backwards, wrenching the jumper around and into, not away from, the cliff.

"Here, that would be fatal," said Carl with raccoon eyes, peering back over the brink.

Just to our left, a striking, 200-foot-high spire canted off the lip like the Tower of Pisa. The most prominent spires along the ridgeline had long before been named after chess pieces. This one was called The Castle, later renamed Stabben Pinnacle, though I never learned why. An exit from the summit, hanging out over oblivion like that, had to be safer than leaping straight off the summit ridge, so it seemed an obvious feature to scout.

Carl hung back as Fred and I scrambled up the Stabben, running with water, to start rock tests. The top was a flat and shattered little parapet. We wobbled a trash-can-sized boulder over to the lip and shoved it off. Five, six . . . *Bam!*—a sound like mortar fire. Debris continued rattling down for ages.

"No good," said Carl, yelling up from the ridgeline. "Way too soon to impact."

We tried again. This time I leaned over the lip and watched the rock whiz downward, swallowed in fog 300 feet below. Three, four . . . *Bam!* My head snapped up. Had to be jutting ledges just below the fog line. We pushed off more rocks and kept hearing the quick, violent impact of stone on stone.

"Forget it," Carl yelled up. "Stabben will never do. It'd be crazy."

The flinty smell of shattered rock lofted up as Fred and I rappelled off the pinnacle and joined Carl.

It took nine more trips to the summit to locate what we knew was the highest possible exit from the ridge—The Bishop, to use the old chess name. For the first time since arriving in Norway, the sky was all blue distance, the entire ridge fantastically visible and spilling down on both sides for thousands of feet. After wandering about up there in the fog during all those scouting trips, it felt like getting paroled to finally see the whole rambling cordillera unmasked like that. We definitely were on the apex, walking unroped on a made-to-order, 10-by-50-foot ledge terminating in an abyss as sudden and arresting as the lip of the Grand Canyon.

Lashed taut to two separate lines, I bent over the drop and started lobbing off bowling-ball-sized rocks while Fred timed the free fall. The rocks whizzed and accelerated ferociously and dropped clean from sight. Twelve, thirteen . . . I looked over at Fred and smiled. This could be it.

Seventeen, eighteen . . . *BANG!* I had to squint to see the puff of white smoke thousands of feet below.

That rock had just free-fallen farther than Half Dome is high. No question, said Carl. The Bishop was our record site. Fred pointed out the original launch spot (or *exit site*), still far left and 300-something feet below. I chucked another rock and we watched it shrink to a pea and burst like a sneeze near the base, the echo volleying up from the amphitheater.

Long story short, a few days later, Carl and his wife Jean, also a skilled BASE jumper, successfully nailed the record jump as a fifteen-person film crew captured it for the then network series, *The Guinness Book of World Records*. It was history. A world record, no injuries. Cameramen raved over the radios. Newsmen and bystanders swarmed the Boenishes after their pinpoint landing. The world toppled off our shoulders. Fred and I were done, and drained. Aside from the weather delays, the show had gone without a hitch, but the crew was scrambling to pack and leave on a charter to Oslo and beyond. The executive producer was so concerned about an accident that he hurried to clear out lest something happen retroactively. The next day, it did.

Carl enlisted two teenage brothers, both local climbers, to hike him up to the summit of Trollveggen. And Carl jumped off Stabben Pinnacle. According to one the boys, Arnstein Myskja, Carl conducted rock tests; in seconds, as before, they smashed off outcroppings jutting directly into the flight path, but Carl was hell-bent on going. As Arnstein later described to me and others, Carl was dead the moment he launched off the lip, or tried to. On his last exit step he stumbled and, unable to push off and get some little separation from the wall, he frantically tossed out his pilot chute. With so little airspeed, it lazily fluttered up, slowly pulling his main chute out of the pack. One side of the chute's chambers filled with air and flew forward. With one side totally deflated, the inflated side wrenched the canopy sharply, whipping Carl around and into the cliff. He continued tumbling down, said Arnstein, his lines and the canopy spooling around him like a cocoon. Five thousand feet later, Carl's tightly wound body impacted the lower slab "and bounced 30 feet in the air like a basketball."

The whole time poor Arnstein was explaining this, trembling in his boots, I kept repeating in my head: "Stabben?!"As a free citizen Carl could do as he pleased, but Stabben Pinnacle? Carl himself had said, "Stabben will never do. It'd be crazy."

Several hours after the rescue helicopter recovered Carl's body at the base of the wall, a local doctor and I moved into the hold of the huge chopper and back to Carl's body, looking like he'd just laid down to get some weight off his bad leg, which he'd shattered in a hang-gliding accident some years before. Regret was nowhere on his face, and the young doctor and I stood there, mourning a life cut in half, gazing from death as if unhurt, but he'd screamed a music too high to scale, and the mountain got him. I was not so selfish to believe it was my doing, but the distance Carl had tracked away from us made me wonder.

I joined the crowd gathering on the grassy field where the copter had landed, all of us looking blankly at each other—someone had to know why and how come. We watched the coroner and two policemen heft Carl's black-bagged body into a white van and roll off into the mist. It felt all wrong to leave it at that, but Carl could not die again. That was all. The end.

Carl's death haunted me for years, and was the first act of a lethal pattern I saw tragically played out far too many times across the adventure sports world: Following a ringing success, a burst of overconfidence lured people—including the very best—to attempt things they had, during sober hours, declared "crazy." Drunk on adrenaline, Carl was like the gambler who changes his betting style. Instead of going with what got him there, which was skill and calculated judgment, Carl listened to that crazy, enchanting voice that said he could do anything. And there's no coming back from that.

Bosom Buddies

If I'm just kicking around, hiking or on a casual mountain bike jaunt, say, I generally go with close friends, and it's a riot. Once the task gets technical, I'm less concerned with bosom buddies than with partnering with someone who can pull their own weight—and mine too if things go south.

Close friends are always first choice. You know what to expect. If you're super active, however, the sheer volume of projects is always more than you can do with just those you know and like. At some point, on a river or slot canyon or wherever you fancy, you'll hook up with people you've only heard about, sometimes with total strangers. We used to see that a lot when tow-in surfing first caught on. The surfers often outnumbered the drivers on the motorized watercrafts, and if you were out on the water and wanted a tow, you'd take one when offered. More than one surfer got towed into a whole lot of trouble, but it usually worked out.

Back when I was an active climber in Yosemite, I sometimes did big routes with foreigners who barely spoke English. Some none at all. It so happened that when two climbers—no matter their differences—both had sights on a particular route up a particular monolith, they often teamed up to accomplish it. It was more business than anything else—at least that's what I thought back then.

Last year I was in Yosemite and was approached by a bearded man who smiled and said my name. Thirty years before, the two of us had climbed a big route on Middle Cathedral, then one of the hardest free climbs in the valley. When I realized the man standing before me was the big Bavarian whose rope I'd shared so long before, we both broke out laughing and spent an hour talking trash and remembering—with waving hands and hack German and English—a day when we both were young, when it had only seemed like business.

BEYOND OUR DIFFERENCES

Back when I was a young climber in Yosemite, the business of eating was paramount. Like all adventure athletes, then and now, we were starving all the time. Food was fuel, and we burned immense amounts of it, judging all meals by quantity, not quality. Whatever money we had, 90 percent of it went to food. Every campsite had a thrashed old picnic table usually shared by six climbers. Every table bore a smattering of pots and pans, black as stovepipes, and an old Coleman stove that broke down so often that every Camp 4 climber knew them as well as their own hands.

Typical meals were one-course affairs. The standard entree was a sort of goulash, consisting of rice and spuds as the principal ingredients, enriched with whatever else we had to chuck into the mix—canned vegetables, tuna, acorns, even pie filling—anything to sweeten the pot. The trick was to keep the stove going and to keep stirring the bubbling gunk so that it didn't burn. Once the fare was judged done, we all tore into it and kept eating till ready to explode. Then we'd rest for a bit, maybe walk a few laps around camp, hitting any peace pipe offered, and then eat some more. And we could always eat more. Or almost always.

A favorite stunt—and I cringe to remember—was to frequent barbecues and picnics put on by various religious groups that swarmed into the park for weekend retreats. These were private gatherings, though strangers were sometimes tolerated so long as the spirit of the thing was close to their hearts (if you could suffer through a sermon and the singing of hymns and so forth). Kind of like the Salvation Army. Acting pious and playing along was our ticket to the chow. So we'd all turn out in our finest red and orange gym trunks, smiling alongside the righteous, the whole while licking our chops and growing increasingly restless till we could finally break for the grub like wolves.

These celebrations were usually large, and our numbers were comparatively so small that we could eat like we'd just stumbled off Annapurna and no one ever cared. Till they did. I've no idea how we learned of these affairs, but the late Alan Bard claimed a tourist couldn't so much as roast a few marshmallows without one of us catching wind of it. We usually tried to keep our numbers down to three or four of our little band, but one time the word had gotten out, and about twenty of Camp 4's hungriest showed up for a stiff affair put on by an old-school Pentecostal church out of Modesto, California.

We were as out of place as arrowheads on the moon, and everyone knew it. This was a humble, low-rent crowd who had little more than pressed jeans, starched T-shirts, and strenuous piety, which violently clashed with the gaudy-colored, devil-may-care hubris of our little band of knuckleheads. The preacher, a nail-thin southern windbag, railed extravagantly about the Good Book, touching on the Eight Visions and Daniel in the Lion's pit, and we wanted to chuck that preacher in there with him, heckled as we were by the smell of those ribs and the fact that he was catching a second wind.

When we finally rose for a closing prayer and the preacher said, "Ah-Men," the climbers stampeded over the congregation and entire tabletops of burgers and fried chicken vanished in seconds. It was like something out of a Fellini film. Climbers plunged bare hands straight into great vats of beans and potato salad, shoveling huge and sloppy loads into their mouths. Punch was swilled directly from the jugs, faces were stuck right into layer cakes and pies, and all this before the proper crowd had eaten so much as a carrot stick. The redneck in many of those present wanted to crush us undertoe. We could see it on their faces. But the spirit was strong, and seemed to freeze them in place, jaws clenched, like bystanders watching a train wreck.

I don't remember what set the thing off, only that one of us crashed the line for the tenth time, reaching for a last drumstick or something, and a deacon angrily grabbed his arm. Words were exchanged; there was some pushing and, as the shocking news spread that the food was all gone, we scattered into the surrounding forest. I had so many franks and ribs and rhubarb pies on board I could barely walk.

Years later, understanding how shamelessly I'd acted in crashing the party, and wanting to make amends, I looked up the old preacher when work took me close to Modesto. The preacher was not so old as I remembered, and his face flushed when I reminded him of that weekend in Yosemite a dozen years before, and that I'd come to make things right if I could. For some reason I thought he'd offer a prayer and forgive me on the spot. Instead I had to return that weekend and spend it sanding and painting and doing yardwork about the plain-wrapped church. I also had to get up in front of the congregation, describe to man, woman, child, and the Holy Ghost the debacle in Yosemite, and ask for their forgiveness. Some of the crowd had been there in Yosemite, and I felt downright corrupt when after the service they pumped my hand and laughed and said it was great I'd come back and come clean and that God works in strange ways sometimes, but I still wasn't forgiven. That wouldn't happen till—at a deacon's request—I hiked the preacher up to Half Dome in Yosemite and got him up the cable route that every summer day tourists march up en masse to the summit. Plus, I had to drive and cover the gas and food for the expedition.

Later that summer we made the summit, though I'm still not sure how because the preacher had a bum wheel and hiked (13 miles up and back) with a wince. We must have stopped twenty-five times for him to massage his leg. On the summit he had a moment, and after some mild probing, explained that during the Vietnam War he'd spent over a year as a POW in the So'nTây prison. The few stories he offered, recited in fragments, with glassy eyes, are better imagined than explained, and curled my hair. Even the good Lord couldn't see him through a few dark nights, when all that sustained him was a childhood memory of camping in Yosemite and an image of Half Dome, floating in the sky like some celestial atoll, a place beyond pain and conflict—and the shrapnel in his leg. That the deacon hoped it might have played out like this is a strange and curious thing.

That might have been my proudest day in Yosemite, summiting Half Dome with the preacher, two people sharing a moment in The Remote, floating in the sky beyond our differences.

CLINT

Just after my junior year in high school I was working on a support raft, carrying all the food and supplies for a dozen or so kayakers making a four-day blast down the Main Fork of the Salmon River. All the boaters were former competitors, except Clint, who had a big reputation for paddling big water, often alone. Most of the others were curious about the man they'd heard so much about, who paddled a banged-up boat and didn't look particularly athletic. More than one (myself included) worried that Clint would hold up the floatilla and was a liability, someone they'd have to watch lest he'd founder.

For this group of experts, the Salmon was more fun than difficult, though they stepped things up by sessioning the hardest stretches of whitewater, each time taking a more daring line down the same water. Clint always managed, but he didn't sport the Olympic posture of the others—sitting noble and upright as the *Artemision Bronze*—nor the powerful, high-handed stroke that made their boats jump forward as if jet propelled. Clint didn't aggressively work a line, like the others; instead he assumed the form of a human cork as the river, it appeared, had its way with him. It was not lost on me, and at first rather fascinated the others, that as they tried progressively more difficult lines—catapulting half the crew from their boats and flipping the rest in turn—Clint never once went over, stalled out, or for that matter, struggled in any visible way.

On the next section of technical rapids, after the team apparently exhausted the possibilities, we all simply watched Clint work four or five additional lines, knifing between wash rocks, rodeoing through haystacks and boils like so much driftwood. The other kayakers, which numbered several national champions among them, couldn't have looked more surprised had Balaam's Ass stroked past on a stand-up paddleboard.

Clint didn't try to impose a perfect stroke or line on his run. He blended with dynamic currents that were far stronger than he was, taking what the river gave him, and worked with that. The idea, said Clint, when asked, is that water itself never got "hung up" or caught in a keeper hole. Rather it flowed right through. Therefore the more Clint could "be like water," not always trying to course correct or maintain "form," the more the river could form his line. He went with what the current gave him, not trying to fight it, but blending. There were fifty corny names that point to what Clint was doing. Not saying he didn't need to avoid obstacles, but not all water on the river flowed into the holes and boils, and he'd try to blend with *that*, and go where that water took him.

As one of the other kayakers later explained to me, competitive kayaking is based on elapsed time and mistakes made. So long as you didn't bang gates, the fastest person won. Take away the gates and the clock and they had a game that was much more Clint's than their own. We all had to see it to believe it.

ONE OF THOSE DAYS

I was working on a film project on the North Shore of Oahu, Hawaii, and got up every morning at sunrise and drove down to the gritty sandstone boulders at Waimea Bay, where I bouldered (practice climbing on short rocks) for an hour till meeting the others for breakfast. I'd read about "The Bay" for years, how in the early 1950s, when big wave surfing first took off, "The Bay" was thought to be haunted by the ghost of Dickie Cross, a surfer, sailor, and paddleboard racer from Honolulu, who drowned at Waimea on December 22, 1943, while attempting to paddle in during a storm. Cross's partner, Woody Brown, was washed ashore unconscious and survived. Dickie's body was never recovered. Fourteen years later, in one of the defining moments in adventure sports, Californians Greg Noll and Mike Strange paddled out into 15-foot Waimea waves and, along with a handful of others who followed them into the lineup, became the first to surf The Bay in big conditions.

Nothing much was happening at The Bay this particular morning, except a violent, 10-foot shore break that would snap a surfer's neck if they ever got near it. The big stuff, the waves people dream and have nightmares about, breaks half a mile offshore, but only goes off a few times a year. There was nothing out there now but a wrinkled gray plane. The beach was empty. Just me and Dickie's ghost as I clawed up the sandy boulders.

I was downclimbing back to the sand when a guy in board-shorts and carrying a boogie board stalked past, glanced my way and snarled, then beelined down to the water. Whatever bothered him had him pretty good. Now the shore break could take its turn. I didn't like his chances.

I forgot about the guy and kept climbing up and down till maybe half an hour later I turned around and there he was, standing on shaky legs and looking a little woozy, with a nasty abrasion over one eye. I walked over and asked, "You alright?"

"Fine," he smiled. "Sorry about earlier. Was having one of those mornings only The Bay could fix."

As Harvey Penick said about golf, adventure sports have probably kept more people sane than psychiatrists.

LIKELY SUSPECTS

I've been around outdoors people for decades, filming them, interviewing notables, writing articles and books about them, sleeping, arguing, fighting, eating, doing about everything I've ever done with the lot of them. In the ways that matter, those chasing high-end adventure sports and those casually venturing into The Remote are the same people—not so much in character, which varies person to person, *but in mindset and intent.*

The big wave hellman is a likely surfer because he grew up at Makaha Beach, or close to Mavericks. Had he grown up in Odessa, Texas, he could just as easily have been a bull rider. Make him an Inuit living on Baffin Island and he might be a polar bear hunter. Put a mix of adventurers in the same room, and you'll see that everyone speaks much the same language.

Anyone with a love for the outdoors can quickly find their people in most any country worldwide. In venturing outdoors, we walk into a fellowship where we *belong*.

PARTNERS

Wolves never hunt alone, but always in pairs. The lone wolf was a myth. Us people *can* go it alone. Most everyone benefits from a solo hike or overnight trip, when we get to reflect and experience self-reliance. The literature is full of inspiring solo adventures, but most of us most of the time will gather into small groups to hike, kayak, and climb. The people in those groups become our partners.

Most partnerships can survive even the worst one-day debacle, but once you start slogging across borders with big loads and no sleep, get pinned down in your tent in a whiteout for five soul-crushing days, or one or the other of you gets the galloping crud when the last ferry is leaving for the mainland and you know you won't make it, the partnership can be made, or broken, forever.

Lasting partnerships are commonly forged between people of similar ages, abilities, likes, and ambitions. A dream shared always feels doable. Yet some of the most durable partnerships I've seen involved odd-couples: the janitor and the linguist, the head-shop owner and the sheriff, the gazillionaire broker and the gardening salesman from Costco. What made these partnerships last, through thick and thin, was compatibility.

Who knows why we get along with some, while others we merely tolerate. There's probably a thousand reasons, and one: hiking that trail, exploring that glacier, skiing that draw is just better with Scarlet, or Billy, or Zoe, than without them. You call Zoe when you hear about a sale on Smartwool socks. Billy reminds you of the time bears got all your food 40 miles into the Appalachians. Scarlet still has your belay device and won't give it back, and that's OK, sort of, because they're your partners. They're who you trust and lean on, hound and endure, give to and borrow from, piss off royally, carry down the trail with a sprained ankle, and laugh with for the stupidest reasons.

Good partnerships are not like no-exit marriages, because you can leave them at any time, but you never really do. You'll likely have more than one partner if you're an inveterate outdoors person. You might have ten, but you'll do your meaningful work with just a couple. As lives unfold, you might not see them for years, but when you do it's like you just crawled out of that muddy cave down in Guatemala—remember that!—and it's time to celebrate.

Partners make a life.

MIKE DOYLE

"They called him Malibu Mike, a tall kid from the wrong side of I-5 who rode the waves (starting in 1953) with a muscular aggression many on the Southern California surf scene had never witnessed," wrote the *LA Times* in a 2019 article. Following his early days in Malibu, Doyle ventured to Hawaii and became an adventure sports icon as one of a handful of pioneers to charge at venues like Waimea Bay, Pipeline, and Sunset, all found along a 12-mile stretch of beach on Oahu's fabled North Shore, the "Mecca of Surfing." While others won more awards, there was a sense within the surf community that Doyle held the soul of surfdom.

His story, transcribed below from a 1998 *Swell Tales* interview, recounts a history, in progression and boundless stoke, that is shared by many adventure sports champions, though rarely with such clarity and humanity. Don't let the smooth tone and easy smile fool you. Mike Doyle challenged some of the fiercest waves ridden during his era, when big wave surfing, as the world now knows it, was essentially invented. Way back when, Mike Doyle wanted to be like Mikey Dora, the Johnny Rotten of Gidget-era surfing. Half a century later, we could hardly do better than to be like Mike.

"I grew up inland, about 15 miles from the ocean. Seemed like a long ways then. First time I got to the beach I was 13. I walked out on Manhattan Beach pier and I saw guys surfing and I couldn't believe it. One guy turned around and actually went backwards, standing on his board. I just couldn't believe it. First time I'd ever seen surfing, hadn't even seen a movie about it—there was hardly any television back then, but to see guys riding a wave was just dazzling to me, looking down from the pier where you could see the trail and the track of water. I knew that was for me the first time I saw it.

"I ran down to the beach and watched them and when they'd lose their boards I grabbed them—of course these boards weighed about 95, 100 pounds and they'd just roll over me, smack into me, had bruises on both legs, just so I could jump on them and paddle about 10 feet out. The guy'd yank the board and say, 'Thanks, kid,' and I'd say to myself, 'I touched one!' I actually touched a surf-board. I was that thrilled by all of it.

"The first person I ever saw surfing was the guy who turned around backward—Bob Hogan. He was a local lifeguard at Hermosa Beach, went to Hawaii every year. And then Greg Noll. He was a skinny kid back then and he could ride forward, backward, and could stand on his head—same Greg Noll we know now who's this big around (big as a barrel). I remember looking in their car and both of them had trophies, for a surf contest and a paddling race, and I went, 'Wow!' I was just a 13-year-old grimme who'd never been on a board before and I see these guys riding on these waves and having trophies in their car—this cool '41 Ford coupe all buffed out—and I said, 'This is the life for me. I wanna be a life guard and go to Hawaii and ride the big surf!'

"When I first got down to Hermosa Beach I got tortured by the in-gang, you know. I was an outsider from . . . they didn't know where. They'd never been east of the I-5 freeway. Years later when I was at Malibu, I had a real lucky deal. My step-father had a job at the Navy base and every day he drove to Point Mugu (10 miles up the coast from Malibu) along the coast highway. Every morning I got off at Malibu, and every evening he'd come back down the coast and pick me back up at 6. Every day at Malibu. All summer long and on the weekends in winter. For most of these guys, during a big swell, Malibu was the place to go.

"They started calling me Tiki Mike back at Hermosa because I made these dumb little tikis in high school. I thought they were cool because I was reading everything I could at the library about surfing and Hawaiians and they all had tikis in their folklore. So I started making little tikis in wood shop. I put them on a leather thong and wore them to the beach and the surfers said they were kinda geeky. They were all wearing St. Christopher's medals. Those were cool. Tikis were lame. Five or six years later (in Malibu) they'd ask, 'Are you the same Tiki Mike we used to know down in Hermosa,' and I said, 'Yeah,' and they said, 'Man, your surfing's getting really good.' I was accepted then as a guy who had talent and had developed in the ranks of surfing. So I turned into 'Malibu Mike.'

"When I first went to Malibu, the guy to copy was Mikey Dora. He had such charisma. The poses and expressions, always had a classic car—a Cadillac or something. He always did artwork on his surfboard that said *Kizzam!* or *Kaboom!* or *Superman.* Every kid on the beach emulated Mikey Dora. The way he walked, the way he talked, and the way he surfed, because he was quite a good surfer. He was real quick and agile and they called him The Cat. Mikey Dora way ahead of his time.

"There was a kind of localism at Malibu. In Ventura there's actual gangs and if you're an outsider they slash your tires and stuff like that. I can't stand that. I've seen it happen in Mexico, too, down in Baja around where I live, and the locals say, "This is our water. You guys are gringos." Or you go to Hawaii and you're a haole. I just don't like racism in any form. I think the ocean should be enjoyed by everybody and respected by everyone.

"My philosophy started pretty simple from my mother, and it still holds true. She never pushed me about becoming a doctor or a dentist or anything. Her main thing was to be a good person, take care of yourself, take care of your health, and do unto others as you do to yourself. It's pretty basic stuff but pretty big stuff. Sometimes the little stuff's big stuff. Try not to cheat and lie because that's the stuff that starts bringing you down. Just tune into yourself and what you can possibly do out there, try and help some other people besides just yourself. It's easy to be greedy. It takes more talent and skill to help somebody else who might not be as gifted as you.

"People ask me, 'Who's the best surfer in the world,' and I say, 'The one having the most fun.' And they say, 'Wow. I thought you were gonna say, Kelly Slater.' And I say, 'No. If Kelly's having the most fun, sure, he's the best.' You should be there to have a good time. Any way you wanna do it. Some people stand on a big board and cruise along and that's great. Other people have to cut real hard and turn and slash and rip off the top of giant waves, and if that's their way to have fun, that's fine too.

"The future? I pretty much see myself doing what I do now: painting and surfing. Live to surf, surf to live."

Stricken with amyotrophic lateral sclerosis (ALS), also known as Lou Gehrig's disease, Doyle stayed in the water all the way to the end. He died on April 30, 2019, at his home in San Jose del Cabo at the tip of Baja California, not far from the perfect curls that seemed to script his life. Mike Doyle was seventy-eight.

"It's a beautiful day here in San Jose, the waves are perfect and we know Mike is smiling in heaven, surfing an endless wave," his wife Annie wrote on his Instagram account.

Performance

PARTICIPANTS AND PERFORMER

Most of us come to the outdoors through an activity. We ski or run trails or bodysurf. Hiking is the most common activity because there's usually some approach march required to get to where we can fly fish or take wildlife photos. Many outdoor athletes began as hikers and scramblers. I did.

The natural progression is to start with modest goals. We want to get outside and burn off some stress. Feel the sun. Get out of Dodge for a moment and reset. Perhaps half of those found on urban trails never leave them. Nor do they want or need to. The other half find themselves meeting people, going on different hikes, extending their trips. Their fitness improves, and their options broaden. Instead of merely putting a few miles on the same old trail, they'll hike for a target, like a peak or the top of a ridge. Next thing they're picking off bigger peaks, then doing so in winter, when an ice axe and crampons are welcome aids. They take a seminar. Join a club or a like-minded group of friends who share a building passion. Their goals expand. They pick up the basics of rope work and the roped safety system, and start doing simple climbing, canyoneering, and more ambitious peak bagging. Before long, what started out as casual strolls in Virginia woodlands, say, has morphed into technical work. However ordinary, they have moved to the fringe of adventure sports, where an aspect of performing is unavoidable.

This progression is repeated millions of times each year, all across the globe—crossing the Maginot Line where participants become performers.

In traditional sports, participants and performers have comfortably coexisted for centuries. If we go to a golf tournament, a majority of the crowd are weekend hackers who come to see the pros perform. We're all entertained, but also inspired. We see the pro tee off and it enlivens our own game.

———

Parasailing is as different from nature photography as trail running is from cave diving. But they're all activities that happen outdoors, and as I've seen over the last forty years, the key factors to performance in any of these (and other) pursuits boils down to a handful of fundamentals.

One common misconception is that performance derives from natural ability. Truth is, no one, however gifted, arrives on the scene with anything close to a complete game. The skill we see in the professional was realized through cultivating fundamentals, but before we can develop anything, in practical terms, certain performance principles must be in place. I call these "required resources."

In looking back at all the adventure athletes I grew up with and have had the pleasure of being around, their backgrounds are as diverse as their chosen sports. Some had money, but most were broke and were too young to earn much income. Some had the support of parents and friends, while others were discouraged from slumming with rogues and daredevils. The kid with a dream always finds a way providing the required resources are available. There are exceptions, but by and large, to be an expert in any outdoor discipline, seven basic resources are required.

1. Ready access to a venue. Nobody becomes an expert diver in the mountains. A diver has to dive, a lot, so you need big water nearby. Most pro skiers grow up near ski resorts. Great surfers live at the beach. You have to have ready access to practice; you have to practice to build skill. None are possible without a suitable venue nearby.

2. A community of players. People of similar skill get paired off into teams and squads, or are naturally drawn together because they share the same interests at basically the same level. Wherever the sport, you see it, live it, dream it, hear all about it. It's the axis around which your life turns, and it turns in the context of a group, however loose or organized, that shares the same passion. Many in adventure sports value independence, but no world-class performer operates with no history or contact with a peer group. That is, no one reaches the top all on their own. You might not rub elbows with the crowd, but you've seen them perform and know what they're doing.

3. Mentors, teachers, and coaches. The younger you get solid instruction, the better. It decreases the chance of learning bad habits you later have to unlearn—a difficult process. Teachers show you what to practice, so the practice is worthwhile. Coaches keep you focused on what is and is not crucial to the game. Mentors and role models show you what a champion looks like, how they embody their expertise. You get a feel for what is required. You see what you need to make your own. You learn the way and the means of the champion.

4. Ability. Who *has* it and who doesn't? The prodigy often burns out or loses interest. The natural's learning curve eventually flattens out. The champion probably started with solid native gifts and through dedication, instruction, and a fertile environment, kept improving. The world champion is likely a person who fell in love with the activity that best suited her basic talents and make-up. This is lucky and rare—that of all the sports and activities out there, you find the one natural to you—which is one reason why there are so few champions.

5. Mindset. No one goes the distance solely on physical talent. Nearing the top, everyone is highly skilled. The champion always has a solid mental approach. No single mental approach fits all. More on this later.

6. Passion. Every champion is passionate, sometimes to a fault. Passion for the sport, the people, the history, the gear, the whole shebang. We will see these played out in many of the entries in this book.

7. Sacrifice. You can't reach your potential if your attention and time are scattered across multiple platforms. The champion likely sacrifices much that is "normal," even essential to what most consider a worthwhile life. Most champions border on the obsessive, which can become its own problem if some balance is not sought and found.

That said, the utility of this review is not to try to live up to it, or adopt it as your personal style—few are interested or inclined to the full immersion and commitment just described, but so long as you understand the principles, you can toggle back to whatever level of dedication seems right for you at a given time. Nobody, even the world champion, can sustain perfect adherence to these principles. Life happens, and there's not always time or energy to go full bore. But while your interest, drive, and dedication may vary over time, the basic principles remain the same. They are what we all come back to, over and over, in our own way.

FIRST DAYS

Rookies get frustrated. They can't get the Eskimo roll, or keep their skis together, and their mask keeps fogging up. They seldom appreciate what they'll never have again: a learning curve as steep as K2.

The more rudimentary your technique, the faster you can improve. I've seen novice mountain bikers, who could barely stay on the saddle in the morning, bombing down singletracks by noon. Once you find your sea legs, the trips start blending together. But you'll never forget those first days, when everything was a discovery.

Yvon Chouinard, climbing pioneer and owner of the Patagonia clothing line, said that becoming an expert was something of a booby prize. During his early years, scratching up the practice rocks in Southern California, every outing felt like the first time, every peak felt like the Eigerwand. The novelty diminished with experience, as he repeated familiar moves and sequences, just in a different setting. As a novice, however, every step was new. It was Christmas every day.

LOVE AFFAIR

I first remember John Bachar as a skinny blond sixteen-year-old with chrome buck teeth, the real ones knocked out in a skateboarding wreck. When John stepped from the track (as a wannabe Olympic pole vaulter) into the So Cal climbing scene, heads turned. Word was that he'd seen an old photo in *National Geographic* of Layton Kor climbing the Titan, and he declared himself a climber before he knew what end of the rope to tie into. It didn't matter how John, or any of us, ever arrived outdoors, only that we had.

John had recently gotten his driver's license and salvaged a 250 Yamaha motorcycle that had caught fire and which John rebuilt in his mother's garage. Most of us lived near a practice climbing area, if only a hillside of small boulders. Not John, who lived close by Los Angeles International Airport. Every afternoon after school he'd nurse the old Yamaha out to the sandstone crags at Stoney Point, in San Fernando Valley (a round-trip of 90 miles from his home), and climb himself to smithereens. In less than a year John Bachar was breaking news in the budding adventure sports movement. Then he broke from the pack.

Ground zero was Yosemite Valley, the Mecca of world rock climbing, where every May, people would stream in from the four corners to take a shot at the great granite monoliths made famous by photographer Ansel Adams.

Back then, "Sam" was a fixture in Yosemite, and one of the first people I'd met there who had genius-level talent, but Sam's flame burned low—like a Brahams or Stravinski, content to play chopsticks.

One afternoon in the Camp 4 (the traditional climber's campsite) parking lot, Sam was complaining to me that he of such marvelous talent hadn't made his mark. Fame meant little to any of us, but Sam hadn't even managed the climbs that could give him prodigious experiences, which was the entire plot. "I just don't know why," he said.

Moments later, John Bachar wheeled into the parking lot on his Yamaha 250, smoking and hissing from his 300-mile journey from LA. The engine fairly glowed. John's throttle hand had gone to sleep back in Bakersfield, he laughed, so he'd taped the throttle wide open and beelined to Yosemite. Nothing could stop him from returning to his Promised Land, just as nothing could stop him on the rocks. John and Sam knew each other as gifted individuals, but their approaches were radically different, something Sam never realized.

John was a generational talent, it is true. His soloing feats were monuments to courage and mastery, but skill and boldness don't explain his greatness. When John first saw that picture of climbers in *National Geographic*, lashed to the side of the desert spire, it was love at first sight. *That's* the reason John became one of the seminal figures in twentieth-century adventure sports and why Sam, for all his talent, never did.

SCORERS

In basketball, they talk about shooters and scorers. A pure shooter has a perfect stroke, and through years of practice can sink an open jumper with uncanny frequency, and she will crucify you in a game of HORSE.

The problem is, shooting only counts in the context of a game, where defenders relentlessly drape and harass the shooter, who rarely gets an open jumper. Unless a shooter can knock down shots in a game, where points count toward winning and losing, form means nothing at all. A scorer knows how to score in the context of a game, accomplished by adjusting his form to what the opponent gives him.

In adventure sports, the "shooter" looks good doing it, is Instagram perfect, but the "scorer" does the meaningful work. She breaks new ground and establishes the classics, which at the time of inception is the cutting edge. The scorer writes the history.

The curious thing is that there's no good road map to becoming a scorer, though there's every reason to want one. Each champion must work it out in their own way. The wisdom is accepting that's so, knowing you'll reach a point, on the far side of the possible, where you can only look inside and hope you find something. The champion feels it and he does it, and no one can really explain it.

ORIENTATION

A dizzying array of books and articles suggest strategies to increase performance. The problem is, specific, regimented approaches can work against you without a clear grasp of the big picture, something few appreciate or understand. In this regard, peak performance coach Brad Stulberg offered the following (paraphrased):

- Reflect on your current level of performance and where you want to be.
- Decide if you want to commit to a state of stress, taking on just-manageable challenges, or a state of rest, recovery, and reflection.
- Align your training accordingly.
- Take a performance inventory every few weeks (crucial for all training programs) and evaluate your progress.
- Make necessary adjustments to your routine.

Without some general orientation, as just described, people often commit to grueling training regiments before honestly reflecting on where they are—physically, mentally, and emotionally. This can lead to burnout, which can derail and even end a promising career. Fruitful preparation works from the big picture to the small details, then toggles back out so you can get your bearings. It's a little like hiking on a trail: We watch our step, moment to moment, occasionally glancing up to check our progress.

FITNESS

The greater degree performance is a factor in our adventures, the greater degree fitness plays a part. Recreational outdoors people sometimes think they can round into shape on the trail, in the cave, or on the mountain. The fact is, most extended trips are wars of attrition, where we inevitably end up weaker than we started. A ten-day beatdown on a mountain trail can melt fifteen pounds off us and take two weeks to bounce back from. Before every expedition I went on (after the first one, when I didn't know better), I worked out like a fiend during the months beforehand and fattened up as much as I could, knowing I'd look like the Thin Man by the trip's end—and I usually did no matter how much we ate.

Whatever fitness level you take into the wilds, count on it diminishing from there. That is, each individual junket leaves us worn out. It doesn't leave us stronger than when we started. Then we rest, eat, recover, and prepare, and return a little stronger than before. It's a strange process when we think about it. We charge a battery, run it dry, recharge it and use it again, but the battery max capacity never increases. Ours can, but not while we're burning though our juice. That means the recovery phase is as critical as the action phase, when we drain our reserves.

Anyone who puts a premium on performance needs to make a lifelong study of these principles. Most performance plateaus result from poor training techniques, rather than reaching a physical ceiling.

NOT FUN

Few work their weaknesses as hard as their strengths. It's not immediately gratifying. It's not fun. It's work. It's stressful and annoying, and we feel like bumblers. Everyone hates that feeling.

So we practice what we're good at, riding only those waves we *know* we can make. Waves where we can shine.

This, second only to fear, is the most limiting syndrome I've found, in myself and others, in a lifetime of venturing outdoors. It warrants a studied look.

Most of our flubs, unintentional dismounts, wipeouts, and so forth typically describe a pattern, and that pattern discloses our weaknesses. If not addressed, weakness leads to fear, and avoiding any adventure that exposes our weakness. This puts many adventures out of reach because the classic dives and runs and mountains and treks are often long and multifaceted, requiring general competence—including the skillset we lack. Some people are fine with this. Accept your limitations. It leads to a balanced life. But if performance is important, avoidance strands even the gifted in shallow waters.

Mastery is not the end-all. Enjoyment and satisfaction are, but it's maddening to keep dodging that downhill course or point break out of fear. What to do? The trick, of course, is to work on our weaknesses. Why is that so hard? Because few understand the basic strategy—to invert our normal inclination, choosing to *first* work on our weaknesses, then later, if at all, touching on our strengths, which need not be learned, merely reviewed. Easier said than done.

For example, early on I hated wide cracks. No part of my body fit into them. It felt like wrestling alligators. I flogged. I grunted, thrutching up an inch and sliding down two, grinding the skin off my knees and elbows. I got my ass whupped so often I swore off "the wide" forever. But every big route in Yosemite featured some wide, often a lot of it. I couldn't climb the big ones on my own terms.

When my frustration from avoiding felt worse than "the wide," I returned to the flared chimneys and off-width cracks— hating every second of it—till finally I started to enjoy them. Fear and bumbling slowly morphed into skill.

This secret sauce is discipline. Working my deficits ran contrary to the way I was made, to avoid stress and seek immediate satisfaction and fun. But over the long haul, avoidance checks freedom. If you want a takeaway from every champion ever born, the common trait is the discipline just described.

WORKING OUR EDGES

Our *baseline* is whatever level of performance we can consistently achieve before our form starts flying apart. Moving past our baseline involves working our edges.

We have a strength edge, a stamina edge, a balance and agility edge, a flexibility edge, a composure edge, an attention edge, a relaxation edge, a breathing edge, to mention a few.

Our weaknesses become evident as we approach our edges. For example, once we reach our relaxation edge (scared), we might start holding our breath (breathing edge). Approaching our strength edge, we're prone to start rushing (composure edge).

Whenever nearing or exceeding our edges, we naturally try to avert our weaknesses by recruiting our strengths. The moment we reach our flexibility edge, for example, it's common to try to muscle our way through.

Useful practice involves pushing the edge of our weaknesses without trying to compensate with our strengths. A handful of basic methods, applicable to all outdoor sports and activities, have been developed to do so.

Below our baseline. Work on technique during easier workouts and warm-ups. When working below our baseline, it's much easier to relax, breathe, and style our way through on balance and agility. Once we can hold form on the easy stuff, we automatically retain that form as we near and exceed our limit.

Beyond our baseline. There is some benefit from occasionally trying things well beyond our max, especially when feeling stuck at a particular level. Be innovative. Dare to try techniques that look and feel unreasonable, even absurd. It's one way to find out what does and doesn't work.

Keep most of your practice near, or just a hair past, your baseline, where your edges are stretched, but not so far that you start using your strengths to compensate. Doing so forms bad (limiting) habits that are hateful to later unlearn.

Vary the pace. We naturally settle into whatever pace is most comfortable to maintain our baseline. The moment we slow or quicken that pace is an eye-opener as it lays bare our performance edges.

When a mountain biker stops bombing down a technical singletrack and slows to a crawl, her balance and agility edge is instantly experienced. When a peak bagger quickens his pace, his fitness edge is obvious in no time.

By *slightly* increasing and decreasing our baseline pace, our edges are slowly expanded.

Boosting pace can prompt rushing and floundering, but slight increases, especially with fast-moving sports, builds agility and helps train our brain to more effectively process information. Borrowing from ball sports, the hardest throwing pitchers all top out around 100 miles an hour. Hitters benefit from setting the pitching machine at 105 mph and taking some practice swings, but cranking the machine up to 120 mph is counterproductive.

Quiet your movement. Sounds simple enough: Don't let your body make excess noise while performing. Eliminate needless motion. Quiet and simplify. It's often been said but it's hard to overstate how helpful this is in building technique and efficiency.

Train with training partners. Going outdoors with friends is a riot, but most any effort to "train" with them usually goes bust, as fun is the aim—as it should be—followed by beers.

To keep focus, train with partners with similar goals, who are there to improve, not socialize.

Never compare yourself with others. Enjoy the process. This attitude brings the best results for the professional and the novice.

Always return to the basics. They're "basic" for a reason. All good technique and performance is built on basic movements.

Basic movements incrementally expand as the sport or activity expands, but the way to improve is almost always to simplify.

Intensity Breeds Champions

What is the single biggest factor that makes a champion? It's a fascinating question. The question makes several assumptions. Any potential champion has the physical gifts, the drive and passion, an available venue to practice a given sport, and sees, first-hand, examples of excellence embodied by other high performers, coaches, mentors, et al. Beyond that, the deciding factor is that *the best train and perform at a higher intensity than anyone else.* The particulars, the *what* and the *how*, have been objectified a thousand ways for each activity, and are covered in endless books and articles, many of those found online. The general principles, however, are tricky to summarize. But let me try.

Sustained activity is not enough. It's the accrued experience at maximum or near-max capacity that forges an ace. This is only possible if you practice smart, which is a learned skill for all involved. You can't simply copy a champion's training schedule because at the outset, the intensity would kill you. You have to work up to it by way of intervals, with appropriate rest to recover. Over time, your baseline fitness and performance keeps creeping up.

Every phase is not an attempt to increase intensity. Some are maintenance cycles. Especially when you plateau. Then you or a coach discovers some new ingredient, some addition, some refinement, even eliminating this and focusing more on that, whatever *that* is, and after another interval of training, you peak at a higher level. But the thing that remains constant is high intensity.

Consistency is key. That's why injuries are a champion's worst enemy—even more reason to train smart because many injuries are sustained during training. A champion is always juggling dozens of factors, trying to bump up performance. It's not an easy job.

As they say in boxing, you never get a belt by beating bums. You need world-class training and champion-level opponents—or deep caves, big waves, huge rocks, steep trails, places requiring intense effort to succeed.

The champions are consistently more active than anyone else. They dive more (for example), study more, watch more video, train more—the champion is a master of *more*, and that *more* is done intensely.

In three words: Intensity breeds champions.

GREAT PERFORMERS ARE COMPLETE

It happened over time and in stages, particularly at Olympic development programs worldwide, where fencers and high jumpers and wrestlers, et al. shared a common facility, and coaches of many disciplines were thrown together and started comparing notes. What they discovered was that athletes in any discipline who focused only on sport-specific skills and training eventually fell behind athletes who augmented their routine with exercises and elements (including the mental game) that had no direct or apparent link to their given sport. For instance, the biathlete who added yoga, meditation, and slacklining into their routine, as opposed to simply skiing and shooting, often left the others behind.

Cross-training has long been part of many routines. The boxer chopped wood, dragged tires (and other kooky drills), and did roadwork, often in combat boots. Once performance cross-training became required practice, and the methods refined, records starting falling like hailstones.

Great athletes are *complete* athletes. Every outdoor activity, from backpacking to backcountry skiing, requires a wide skillset. The expert in any discipline is she who has mastered the overall game, mostly from working on her weaknesses. In adventure sports, the champion became one through seeking a complete game, continually building on the four pillars of athleticism: movement, mindset, nutrition, and recovery. Each of these is a lifelong study. Something as basic as periodization is far too complicated and nuanced for a nontechnical book like this, but it's exactly such factors that craft a complete, modern athlete. Also, what worked for you at twenty-two won't work at forty-five. Performance is a game of constant adjustments. We live in fine times when useful information about every aspect of the process is readily found.

The aim of reviewing a champion's approach is not to try to be one. Few of us have the gifts to ever get close. Few with the talent choose to sacrifice most all semblance of a normal life, whatever that is, to chase a single dream, with little chance of seizing it and no chance of holding it for long. Since performance is meaningful to most of us, we benefit from reviewing effective means of improving. It's no fun being crappy at something we love. Improving is intensely gratifying, for everyone at every level.

Even this is not a blueprint for all. Take what you want and leave the rest.

ONE THING AT A TIME

The exercise, in 150 words: Whatever the activity, intentionally pay attention to one component of the overall game. A mountain biker might single out body position, and stay with the exercise for a couple rides, making small adjustments on things she'd never noticed before. Focus on whatever you normally do unconsciously. You might be surprised with how much that involves.

When you become aware of form breaks, move to correct them. Many form breaks are composite mistakes, so you again pick out one aspect and work on that. It's nearly miraculous the rate of improvement this simple exercise can accomplish, as well as the novelty it can bring to the same old activity, typically done on autopilot.

Eventually you start observing larger pieces of the total movement, till the whole process dovetails into flow. As it goes with most everything mentioned in this book, we have to bring awareness to the game before change is ever possible.

Go to Failure

Climbing guide Bob Gaines had a knack for squeezing performance out of beginning students. His motto: Go to failure. Or, give yourself a chance to succeed. Both say the same thing.

Beginning rock climbing students start on short walls with a rope belayed from above, every inch of slack taken up as they climb higher. Should their grip fail or a foot blow off a hold, they "fall" no more than a foot or two, directly onto the rope. Properly arranged, the risk approaches zero.

First-timers never want to fall because they don't trust the system, but even some advanced climbers grab gear or hold onto the rope rather than climb till they fall off, even when there are no apparent risks.

For some it is a control issue. More frequently it is a fear of failure. Gaines's method was to feed out slack whenever someone did or attempted to grab the rope (used strictly as a safety device— it is cheating to use for upward progression). He wouldn't lower a student off till she fell off the climb.

Clients were amazed that when they were willing to try till they fell, they oftentimes never did. Providing the safety margin is acceptable, because the person who stops before failure is settling for too little. You're placing a performance limit on yourself before you know where your limit lies. If the consequences of failure are known and acceptable, give yourself a chance to succeed. Go to failure. It's the quickest route to performance.

Perfect Turns

I recently read an article about Olympic and World Cup skiing champion Mikaela Shiffrin, whose race of choice is slalom, which is all about turning.

During the season there are roughly fifteen slalom races, each lasting less than two minutes. All told, Mikaela might race slalom half an hour throughout an entire season, and yet she's continually on the snow, practicing.

Every champion has mastered competing, but the right to compete at the World Cup level is won through practice. Her parents and de facto coaches taught Mikaela to practice refining her turns even when skiing to the chairlift.

Her father, Jeff Shriffin, said, "One of the things I learned from the Austrians is: Every turn you make, do it right. Every turn counts."

Few of us venture outdoors seeking perfection, yet most of us have particular skills that hold special value and importance. Develop the discipline to do those "right." They're the ones that count.

TRYING TOO HARD

About six of us decided to put aside climbing and surfing and everything else and concentrate on mountain biking for one solid year, to see where we might take it. James had the most talent in our little group, but instead of going for long rides with the rest of us, where the whole process might come together for him (as it slowly did for us), James would stop and binge ride the hardest section of a given trail, rarely completing the whole thing. In a few months we all passed him by, and nobody understood why. How could the best among us continually practice the hard stuff and get left in the dust by riders of less ability? That took some time to unpack.

Yes, the champion is she who trains and performs at the highest intensity, but this is a learned skill, something the pro slowly worked up to. When the pro's performance dips or tanks—as happens to the best of them—they dial down the intensity to discover the problem and work out the bugs. An aspiring expert like James had never developed expert prowess, and was so overmatched by professional-level courses that he never developed the feel of mastering what he *could* do, never locked into the flow, never learned to put it all together. He just kept getting bucked off on 6-foot drops and hairpin turns. It's amazing he didn't kill himself trying. When James finally toggled back to easier ground and found his rhythm on then-doable singletracks, he worked up the ladder in no time.

There is some benefit to trying things too hard for you, but progress is usually easier, faster, and less painful through mastering the levels equal to your current ability. Strangely, we tend to improve in fits and starts, and not on things that have always been too hard. Rather the stuff at our actual level suddenly starts to feel casual. *Then* we step it up.

LESS IS MORE

Modern adventure athletes start younger, get better instruction, train smarter and longer, eat better, and are continuously raising performance standards. The equipment is better, the routines more advanced, and the competitions for every adventure sport are more frequent and well organized. All these factors have hastened the evolution. Yet the basic game remains the same. The waves at Jaws (a legendary big wave break on Maui's North Shore) are just as big, and people still get tired.

Several years ago we were filming in Yosemite, and Carlo Traversi—one of my favorite people on earth, and a rare talent—had climbed for five days straight and decided to do *Astroman*, "The World's Greatest Free Climb" back in the 1980s and '90s, now relegated to a trade route for aspiring experts, but still long and strenuous, top to bottom. I suggested to Carlo that he take a rest day, and he chuckled that we'd done that climb decades ago and that he'd manage. So we strung 1,400 feet of fixed ropes, set up the cameras, and watched Carlo flame out just a few rope lengths from the bottom.

Nobody has unlimited endurance. Carlo could have hiked that route if he were fresh, but after a five-day beatdown, a forty-year-old-route spanked him handsomely.

The more highly tuned the athlete, the greater the need for rest and recovery. If your game is intensity, less of your best stuff is often more. We aren't machines.

Curiosity

Top performers, and those who wring the most enjoyment from their outdoor pursuits, often share a common trait: curiosity. They are people naturally inclined to stay with problems a little longer than the rest of us, who simply want to get on with things and can't be bothered dogging down the fine points. The aficionado thrives on what most of us consider boring—the reading up on, the analyzing, the comparing, the journaling, the constant conversations with others about minutiae that would put a corpse to sleep.

I once asked a legendary explorer how she could keep reading all those books and watching so many videos. She surprised me by saying she was trying to know what the hell she was doing. This from a woman who'd tromped to both poles, had traversed New Guinea, and was off to Mali as soon as she got it all straight in her head. Thing was, she wasn't afraid of what she didn't know, ergo all the research.

"If I knew what I was doing," she said, "it wouldn't be called research."

That's hardly a straight answer, but you'll see that curiosity in most any outdoors person who knows what they are doing.

Travels Well

The advantages of traveling to new areas and embracing new challenges and foreign conditions are not immediately evident, especially when you spend precious time and money questing to a new break or backcountry skiing venue and the whole thing goes bust. The waves are garbage. The snow is crap. You've wasted your time.

Not so fast . . .

The occasional player, the dabbler, is best served by sticking with established, go-to areas, where the chances of finding the gold are high, but for the person into an outdoor pursuit for the long haul, there's more to it than the quality of a given place. This takes a little explaining to understand.

Every trip into The Remote is a step into the unknown because even if we hike the same path, weekend after weekend, the conditions are constantly changing. Heraclitus knew as much when he said, "You cannot step into the same river twice." The trail in July heat is a whole different animal in a December snowstorm. But in fundamental ways, we're still covering the same ground.

The Remote is sure to broaden our perspective by way of varied experiences, but by sticking too closely to old hunting grounds, to the same dives, rivers, caves, or canyons, we groove our experiences into a sameness that limits the sparkle most seek outdoors. Problem is, few of us favor the new over the tried and true, especially if we have limited time and opportunity to get our adventure on. Why risk going to X, which might be a bust, when we can return to Y and cash in. So most of us play it safe and go where the money is, to the proven spots. No harm in that—unless performance is a priority.

With track and field, say, where the events are uniform, every track and every field is basically the same, and records have been set on many of the good ones, but with most outdoor pursuits, where every wave and every climb and every cave is different, staying close to home will at best produce a specialist who, like wine, doesn't travel well. That's why professionals and weekend warriors continually visit new areas. The wider our curriculum, the wider our skillset. Encountering new areas and challenges is also the best way to keep things fresh, stay motivated, and avoid burnout. The main reason to keep going far afield concerns performance.

We all love, for example, the perfect wave and the diamond hard rock, but we don't always get it, even in Yosemite or at Sunset Beach (a favored Hawaiian break). Pro surfers often compete on crappy, windblown waves, and that's when all those sessions at the foreign area, infamous for riptides and choppy combers, pay off handsomely. And most any big climb is sure to feature some wet and mossy rock. If we've limited our experience to those places where the getting is always good, our performance will likely tank when it's not. The expert is solid in all conditions, because that's what she's used to. You get the point.

If we want to perform, we have to mix it up. We might think little of half the new places we visit, but only if our criteria for "good" is perfection. Time spent grappling with bad conditions in second-rate venues will eventually pay off. Every venue won't sparkle, but we might, no matter where we go, because our game "travels well."

Failure

"The champion never fails," was a common refrain I used to hear as a kid. I learned it wasn't remotely true, especially with outdoor adventures, where storms and avalanches, even pesky birds—can thwart the expert and her best-laid plans.

The humility I first saw in a mountaineer like Reinhold Messner, questionably the greatest of all time, was in large part fashioned through his failures, in knowing that his victory in soloing Everest without bottled oxygen, say, was far less a conquest than a narrow escape.

The smug adventurer shows disrespect for reality; often his days are numbered. The champion knows that it's better to turn back than to forge on when the odds are stacked against them.

The most valuable skill is the ability to gauge those odds, a paradoxical knack often learned from befriending failure. Bad failures are when we pushed too hard in the wrong direction, quite possibly got hurt, and the game was canceled forever. The fruitful failures probably left us impatient, but delivered information that later proved useful.

In the world of invention, most any major discovery was preceded by years of failed experiments, each winnowing the possibilities toward the eventual solution. Look for the insights that are by-products of failure. You're going to fail, a lot, if you're pushing your limits.

The champion learns the most from her failures. The hacker keeps making the same mistakes.

DO THE CLASSICS

Mountaineering, as a sport, dates back to the 1854 ascent of the Wetterhorn (Grindelwald, Switzerland) by Englishman Alfred Wills. As the sport progressed, other peaks were climbed in succession, and the best of these were deemed "classics."

Every outdoor pursuit and adventure sport has birthed a slew of classics: downhill biking Bolivia's "Death Road"; cave diving the cenotes (sinkholes) in the Yucatán Peninsula (Mexico); kite surfing at Kailua Beach on O'ahu, Hawaii. The list is endless.

The classics point the enthusiast toward the best a given pursuit/sport has to offer (tending toward the older, less demanding venues), while providing the essential coursework for the aspiring expert. By working through the classics, we have a metric off which to judge our abilities, while completing our basic training in the craft. Every classic presents a new set of challenges, adding to our skill and experience. Once we've "ticked" the modern bucket list, the future belongs to us.

Whatever our goals or aptitude, the classics are the motherlode. For many, rafting the Grand Canyon or hiking the John Muir Trail is the defining moment in their outdoor career, a seminal event they can always come back to and declare, if only to themselves: I was there. I did that. I exist.

LOW ROLLER

For avid outdoors people, weekend adventures keep our stoke alive, but our dreams are usually realized during extended trips of two or more weeks, as funds and schedules allow. The problem is usually money. Not just to get out there, but to sustain yourself at a high level. Not everyone has a $50,000 Sprinter Van tooled out like a suite at Shutters, with cozy beds and a workable kitchen. Camping out and cooking over a stove can keep the costs down, but if you're pushing your limits, camp food, no matter how fresh or expertly prepared, is a long way from the lavish buffets offered to pros on professional sports teams. Pro sports are a business, the athletes are the product, and the athlete's value is based on their performance. Professionally prepared food is not merely a perk or a luxury, but is geared to boost performance. If camp food cooked over a stove set in the dirt improved performance, you better believe they'd go with that.

Makeshift meals, or trying to live off grape leaves, pumice, and veggie dogs, will erode your performance over the long haul. You have to get some quality calories down the hatch to continually perform at a high level, and the trick—refined over generations by millions of outdoors folk—is to know where the food deals are. Locals and regulars always know where. Ask around and learn. Especially at destination areas where the skiers, surfers, hikers, and all the rest go for action, visiting the go-to restaurants and food joints is part of the adventure. It can also extend your trip by helping to make your money last a few days more.

CROSSING THE LINE

In every adventure sport I've tried or seen there's a line beyond which everything, quite suddenly, gets real (read: *serious*). The actual difficulty might only be a tick above your comfort zone, but the first time a climber casts off on a genuine big wall, the first time a solo sailor points his skiff toward open ocean and loses sight of land, the first time a surfer paddles into Mavericks when the waves rear overhead like drive-in movie screens, the intensity, commitment, and consequences for a major form break make the venture feel like chaos. This is heady stuff for everyone, and there's no reliable way to know—*Am I ready?* Not till you cross the line.

Few among us jump straight into the big time without a few speed wobbles. As Swiss downhill champion Beat Feuz said of the notorious Austrian downhill course known as the *Streif* (streak, or stripe), nothing can *fully* prepare you beforehand for such a challenge, but there are proven methods to gauge your readiness before throwing all the marbles. What do your peers, mentors, and coaches—should you have them—realistically think of your current abilities? How do you compare, mentally and physically, with those who have successfully met the challenge? If you're lucky, you can tackle the big time as a team, with experienced hands doing the heavy lifting. At any rate you can stay close to others who have been there before, but at some time you will find yourself with essentially no backup but your own preparation, desire, and native stuff. And you'll never know how you'll react till you're over the line.

Unfortunately, *crossing the line* is not like becoming a citizen. It's not a one-time affair. The first time is most significant because we're passing a psychological barrier we're never certain we can manage till we do. Only later do most of us learn that doing something once never guarantees a free pass next time around. Or ever. How many times have we seen a champion boxer half-ass his training and lose his belt to a better prepared opponent? Or a backpacker, who's let their fitness flag, jump onto a grueling thru-hike and get spanked?

Crossing the line that first time is a confidence builder, but it can never excuse us from the hard work and commitment that got us there. What's more, as we work up the ladder, every rung presents another line to cross. It might never feel as significant and mentally challenging as the first one, but each step forward will require effort to succeed. Most of us reach a level beyond which the effort just doesn't seem worth it. It might also be impossible. The champion is the person who never accepts a limit on their performance. Everyone has one, of course, but the moment we accept one, the podium belongs to someone else.

At the top end, the game goes beyond fun in every direction, but the thrilling dynamic of crossing the line, wherever that is for us, remains basically the same for all.

Poise

MEDICINE

Adventure is medicine, especially the high-end stuff, where the risk is stout and the effort grueling. No one can sustain this indefinitely. You can keep discovering how much more you can do, which is part of the curriculum, but at best it's a zero-sum game. Everyone has a limit.

When I was sixteen I begged my way into a job with Henry Felaney's White Water River Expeditions, which ran raft trips down the Colorado River as it coursed through the Grand Canyon. One time we husbanded a group of kayakers on a nine-day venture, ferrying all their gear on a motorized pontoon raft as they tumbled through Hans, Crystal, and Lava Falls, and all the other storied rapids that make the Grand so formidable.

Lake Powell was swollen from a wet winter and several recent storms, so on the afternoon of the third day, they opened the flood gates on Glen Canyon Dam and the rapids roared like tsunamis. The kayakers were among the best in the business, but the roar was so loud and the action so unrelenting, half the squad wanted to ride in the raft—but it was full of gear. No room for passengers. Several times, when the shorelines converged into narrow canyon walls, guys went over and got washed from their boats and rode the wild current for miles before we could fish them out downriver. It was a knackered, waterlogged crew who scratched from the Grand a week later.

At the take-out at last, one of the paddlers crawled from his boat and walked up to the dirt parking, where his girlfriend was waiting in a Jeep. He simply got in and they drove off, leaving his boat and paddle and all of his fellow paddlers—and 200 miles of whitewater—behind.

Too much medicine.

STRENGTH

Rudy was a local kid from Chatsworth, California, who'd follow us around the boulders and sandstone outcrops at Stoney Point, a popular practice climbing area since the late 1930s. Rudy had the strongest fingers we'd ever seen, but his technique was awful. He naturally tried muscling up problems requiring touch, balance, and finesse. When he'd fail on a knobby face or a crack, he'd bolt back home to work out harder and close the gap. If only he could get stronger, he said, nothing could stop him. He ignored suggestions to practice on the slabs and refine his footwork, to downclimb the easier problems to build balance and skill. Technique meant nothing; strength alone was key. Rudy was certain of it.

Eventually, Rudy's body started cracking from the strain of his workouts. He'd show up at Stoney with a finger taped, a wrist wrapped, sometimes having to climb one-handed because an elbow was yelling uncle. Not surprisingly, his technique and performance improved when he couldn't move solely on power. He had to use his feet, rely on balance and flexibility, which he had in abundance. Yet the moment that throbbing elbow or tweaked finger healed up, he hit the workouts harder still, triggering an injury cycle that ended his career at age twenty-two.

He wanted to be Satriani, but the strings broke.

TEACHING

Colette was one of the finest communicators I was ever around. She shared more than information, rather the love for the whole process and all involved, especially the students. The best teachers have a passion for learning, which rubs off on the rest of us.

Skilled coaches and teachers do not impose. They listen, watch, sense into people and things, and gently respond. The response is more of an invitation than instruction, though for things outdoors, good coaching contributes to a person's safety, performance, and enjoyment.

Technique is most easily learned when it's fun, or at least made interesting. Safety concerns are valued when they're seen to promote enjoyment, but what stays with people is when the teacher-student relationship is itself an enriching experience, regardless of what you learn or how well you perform.

Without a generosity of spirit, the teaching goes into your head, where it's often forgotten. When it's personally offered as a gift, as a part of the coach herself, it's stored in your soul, where it can never get lost.

SAMMY GLARED

Scott was one of the finest climbers of the generation right after mine. He drank too much, argued too much, scrapped with girls too much, was cranky and volatile, but we loved him anyway because he was huge-hearted, smart, and loyal, even when he hated your guts. He was also a highly skilled guide, when he felt like it.

Scott and I sometimes taught Rock 1 seminars for Bob Gaines and Vertical Adventures. Each class typically had at least one challenging student who provoked and pestered and flew into fits. That was Sammy. In spades. Sammy was recently paroled for shooting nuns and orphans, I told Scott, who knew I was lying. Either way, Sammy was now our problem.

Sammy was about twenty, had so many piercings he looked like he'd dived head first into a tackle box, and resembled a welter-weight boxer looking for a fight. I have no idea how he ended up in our class or who brought him. Once we went over the basics, it was time to tie into the rope with the knot we just taught everyone.

Sammy sneered and said, "I ain't doing nothing." Scott saw my face screw up, pushed me aside, and said, "I got this."

Scott walked straight over to Sammy and said, "Whatever you do, don't touch that goddam rope." Sammy immediately grabbed the end of the line, twirling it in the air and smiling, and Scott said, "Don't even think about tying in." Sammy did so in nothing flat. He'd been paying attention after all. Scott fumed, stepped up to the slab over which the safety rope ran. He reached up and grabbed a big letterbox hold and told Sammy, "I better never see you grab this bucket with your right hand." Sammy strode over and slapped his mitt on the letterbox hold.

"You put your left foot on that knob and stand up on it," said Scott, "and we're gonna have words."

Sammy was on it in a second. A few minutes later, having done everything Scott ordered him not to do, Sammy had mastered the slab (rare for beginners), and when I lowered him back to the ground the others students gave him an ovation.

Sammy glared at the other students and said, "Fuck you."

A girl, slender as a reed, who looked like Thora Birch in *Petunia*, took a step toward Sammy, put her hands on her hips and said, "You're not tough. You're miserable."

"He's got every right to be," said Bob, whose timing was always just so. "Just ask him."

Petunia looked right at Sammy and said, "Well, do you?"

"Not really," said Sammy, and laughed. He was also, almost certainly, lying.

Half the champions have a big streak of Sammy in them. When a coach, mentor, or peer group (comprised of so many Sammy's and Samantha's themselves) is not scared off and instead can help him or her focus their energy on an appropriate challenge, watch out. The person on the podium is often a Sammy who learned how to smile, because he was finally given the chance to do so.

And you better believe they earned it.

BETTER BE TOUGH

For much of its length, Highway 140 tracks the banks of the Merced River, on its way to Yosemite Valley. In early spring, fed by snowmelt in the High Sierras, the Merced rages like the Ganges in flood.

In the long winding stretch from Incline up to El Portal, the last small town before the park, you can look left across the rapids at the old stage road, now overgrown, caved in here, washed out there. Just above the road are scattered houses, abandoned ages ago. A mountainside rises just behind this land of ghosts, so you can't access the old road from the other side.

There is an access point, just below El Portal, and though I'd never heard of anyone even walking down the old stage road, the idea was curious, especially to Rex, a friend, avid mountain biker, and bartender at the Yosemite Lodge.

Rex wanted to mountain bike the length of the old road, checking out the abandoned structures along the way. He invited me and Jim Bridwell along. How, Jim wanted to know, did Rex propose to get back across the river once the ride was over, or when the old road ran out. No problem, said Rex. Every 4 or 5 miles there were steel bulwarks on both sides of the river, with a cable strung between and a one-man cab on rollers (chained to the bulwark) so state workers could cross the river that way. Rex planned to take climbing gear along, including a harness, a few slings and a pulley, and so equipped, ride the cable across with his bike.

Jim insisted we try out the escape strategy on the nearest cable, to make sure we couldn't get stranded on the wrong side of the river. Rex couldn't be bothered, so he hit the old road by himself.

A few days later we ran into Rex at the village store. He looked worked. He had pedaled some 25 miles down the old road, he said, checking out the old houses as he went, finding a load of trinkets and heirlooms—including an antique pocket watch, which he showed us—till the road became unridable down by Incline.

Turns out all the bulwarks were faced with a welded grate he could climb around, but not with his bike. Night was already on him and he hadn't brought a headlamp or a coat. Darkness in that canyon is true darkness, so he couldn't reverse course without risking a plunge into the river. He hunkered down and nearly froze to death waiting for morning. He laughed when he said so, winding the pocket watch, but I swore his teeth were still chattering.

Bridwell chuckled and said, "If you're gonna be stupid, you better be tough."

BURNOUT

With standard burnout, your motivation flags and you feel mentally and physically exhausted, usually from too much training stress coupled with too little recovery. You've over-revved your motor and it needs to cool down. When this happens, as it does at some time for most outdoor athletes, don't try to push through it. You'll only get injured. Or kill your stoke forever.

During a serious burnout, most feel an aversion to skiing or climbing or whatever the sport, and wonder if they'll ever rekindle the fire. The best remedy is to get away from the activity and put it out of your mind. Find other interests. The mountain or the trail isn't going anywhere, but you have to for a while. Don't try to schedule a return date because it might never come.

Hall of Fame running back Gayle Sayers said that every player, regardless of age or level, should always "prepare to quit." That is, we must be mentally prepared for the realities of quitting, and for focusing one's energy on the next phase of life. We usually bounce back from early burnouts. Ones later in life often signal an unconscious need for change. What Gayle Sayers said.

"Quitting," as many discover, often means dropping out of performance mode, getting away for a while and returning as a participant, going when you feel like it, or not. For many former champions, these are the best of times, when the game is for fun and fellowship. You might even stoke the old embers here and there. Everyone does it differently.

I Hate This!

We are spiritual beings, some insist, looking toward the sky, unaware that the big silence we find in The Remote is for many the sound of God. Either way, we don't so much learn how to *be* outdoors, as remember.

Scads of good people would rather not. Youth offenders court-ordered into wilderness correctional camps and programs are sometimes transformed. Adults are far less flexible, and if their values don't include some dirt, sweat, and tears, forcing this on them can backfire, hard and fast. Who hasn't seen the man or woman finagled onto the trail or into the cave only to say, *I hate this!* And what of the person who insists that they go with it, that they don't know what they're missing. Wrong. They know exactly what they're missing, and it ain't there.

The Remote is for everyone, but not everyone belongs there.

Don't

Drag an entitlement complex into The Remote and you'll be a liability to yourself and everyone around you. People weaned on instant gratification and overscheduled childhood activities come to expect the world to pay them privileged attention. Their wish is the world's command. Maybe so for the dude in the bistro. But out in The Remote, the daddy-o and the bum are equals.

If you expect Nature to meet your desires you're in for a long adventure. Or a short one.

Always Play for Something

Golfers, bowlers, pool players, and others often play for money because they concentrate more. Plus these sports are more exciting when there's skin in the game, even a few lousy bucks. Go to a horse race and simply observe. It's just a few athletic ponies speeding around the track. Put $20 on Old Rosebud and you're jumping up and down when, "Down the stretch they come!"

Adventure sports give all the stimulation of a horse race, with big money riding on the outcome, and they give it all for free.

When it's not just cash riding on the outcome, but our skin and bones, everyone concentrates. And the thrill is never gone, no matter how hard or how easy.

Service

Some years ago a small group who called themselves The Congregation operated out of a hardware store in Trancas, a ritzy beach village just north of Malibu on Pacific Coast Highway. The Congregation numbered several dozen and looked like a casting call for a pirate movie. So far as I know, they never held proper church services or even had a minister. Their entire mission was community service. I had lunch with a member of the parish, the "Right Deacon Billy" (they had fun with their titles), and interviewed him, recording the conversation on my phone. Said Billy:

"None of us had the dough to live in Trancas. We just worked there. Around ten of us at first. We kept seeing each other at the sandwich and burrito dives around town at lunch. Some of us known each other from recovery programs. Others met at sober living houses near the village there. Couple three were on parole. Maybe more. We didn't have much in common by race or background or other stuff but we all wanted to stay outta trouble and mostly jail. We had our programs, like I said, but since we was always around Trancas we reckoned maybe we could get something going on our own. But had no idea what.

"So we start meeting in the back of a hardware store where High Abbess Shelia works. We read stuff and talk all about it and it don't go nowhere. We tried other stuff that didn't work neither till Linda she says, 'Service. We could start doing something for peoples around here.' 'Cept nobody's sure what.

"We start talking about what everyone does. Hal works in a bike shop. Sid's a welder. Hank also works in metal fab. Caesar, he's an upholsterer. Craig works for the park service. Jules is a janitor at a rehab place for people with spinal cord injuries, and Jules's got some stories. Folks pile up their motorcycle or fall off a ladder and they're paralyzed. Jules, he works swing shift, when the peoples are supposed to sleep but often they can't. He talks to some and they're scared and lose hope. These peoples are already past all the surgeries and hospitals. So now it's just learning how to live with no feeling in their legs and such. The therapy helps and the programs too but the staff are mostly gone at night so the peoples just stare at the ceiling and wonder, What now?

"Jules says once a week they take the peoples who can't walk down to the beach in a big van and plunk them down facing the ocean, and the breeze and sun lifts their spirits. And that's how Sherrill gets the idea that we can take these peoples outdoors, but how? We'd have to carry them. Or just wheel them around in a chair which is better than nothing but not so much.

"Not sure but I think it was Craig who says, 'We wheel them up to Sandstone Peak' (in the Santa Monica Mountains, 10 miles inland from the coast). It's a mile from the turnout and it follows an old fire road to a huge vista. That sounds great, but there's no way a regular wheelchair is going up that road, says Craig. It's plenty wide but it ain't been driven on for years and is rutted and rocky in a few parts. And pretty steep for short bits too. Anyhow Craig runs the idea past the spine joint and they're open to the idea, but only after we show them how it's safe. The problem is the wheelchair. But it's only a problem for like a week because everyone's into it.

"Hal works in the bike shop and gets these huge, balloon mountain bike tires on big bomber rims. Craig borrows a wheelchair from the spine joint and Sid and Hal weld up an aluminum super chair. When they strap on those big tires you could push that rig across a stream bed easy. Caesar sews up some cushions, so the ride will be smooth like and comfortable. Regular wheelchair has little pissant tires up front but Sid and Hal, they's welded up a regular roadster, with those fat ass tires front and back so we's ready to rock and roll.

"First trip up that trail and we only get a hundred yards. Shelia, she's sitting in the chair like a dummy, shouting orders and

Hank, who used to play football and is big as a horse, he's pushing his brains. But it's some loose ground on that trail and steep in parts and Hank is bushed in no time. The rest of us can barely push the chair 50 feet before we drop. So Sid, he welds a mount on the back of the chair so's you can slip in a 6-foot rod he stole from a synagogue where his brother works. Hal, he puts hand grips on the rod and that way three of us can push the chair at once, one person in the middle, and one on each side.

"Now that works like a charm but even so it kicks your ass after a couple hundred yards. So now we gots two teams, and they switch off every five minutes and that ways we get that chair up to the overlook in less than an hour. It's looking real cherry—till we start down. At the first steep bit the chair gets away from us and Shelia has to dive for it and the chair goes tumbling, but it's okay. But Sheila's got scrapes and shit all over, and if she'd been one of them paralyzed peoples we'd be in jail. So good on us for working out the bugs first thing.

"Craig, he strips a disk brake setup off a mountain bike that had fallen off somebody's car rack on the freeway and is ruined, but the brake's fine. Hal welds it all together and Sid rigs the brake handle on the middle of the push bar and that works swell so we're set. Now all we gots to do is prove it to the spinal joint that we ain't gonna kill nobody. Anyhow we gets an administrator and wheel him up to the vista and ease him back down real slow, and he loves it. Next weekend we take our first person on the ride, a girl who broke her back in a horseback riding accident. Things went really well. Most of us hadn't done much right in our lives but we done that right. That girl, couldn't have been much over fifteen, she was floating on a cloud. Couple days later we push another person up to the overlook, and it just sorter took off from there."

The Sunset Gathering, as it came to be known, had been up and running for most of a year when some friends and I first came across the group while hiking out of Echo Cliffs after a day's climbing. Craig, Hal, Sid, and Caesar had fashioned another two off-road wheelchairs, so three patients from the rehab facility enjoyed the ride and were up on the overlook. The group, which numbered eighteen pushers and a half dozen others, had made this trip enough times to time things out so they arrived at the vista overlook shortly before sunset.

As it often happens, much as those who could no longer walk were delivered by their adventure up to Sandstone Peak and the fun romp down the fire road under headlamps, it was The Congregation who were saved in the process. The Sunset Gathering went on for a while longer, but soon there were issues about user permits and insurance and they had to stop the whole thing later that first summer.

Over the years I've seen the outdoors used as a staging ground for everything from executive team building seminars to Kundalini yoga classes. I'm sure good things came out of most of these efforts. But if anyone ever put The Remote to better use than the Right Deacon Billy and his band of pirate saints, I've yet to see it.

BREATHE!

Fritz Perls, founder of Gestalt Therapy, famously said, "Fear is excitement without the breath." This intriguing statement reminds us that the same process that produces excitement also produces fear. When we consciously relax and breathe, fear and anxiety start morphing into excitement. On the other hand, excitement quickly turns into fear when we hold our breath.

Most adventure sports require athleticism, explosive strength, fine motor control, and usually, a ton of balance and agility, all of which are challenging to execute in concert, into a flow. Add risk and fear into the mix (often the case) and breath-holding is common, even instinctive. So for most, relaxed performance breathing is an acquired skill that at first they have to practice as a specific exercise. Most people pick it up quickly. Those who don't need only extend the exhale, and the rest will follow.

By consciously doing breath checks while performing (only takes a second), we reverse our tendency to anxiously tighten up as we approach the hard part, or start to get tired. Once periodic breath checks become habitual, so too does deep, relaxed breathing that's connected to the movement itself, even in the heat of battle. Mottos like "Relax through it" are sound advice, but almost worthless without a method. The method is to *breathe through it*. Everything follows from there.

WIND!

Sailors and kite- and windsurfers thrive on wind so long as it doesn't pass a threshold that turns those sports into survival drills. Biking with a stout tailwind is sensational; turn that bike around and we're hating life. Wind is especially irksome for rock climbers. Hands and faces go numb in temps below about 55 degrees F, as the ropes kite so far left or right you'd swear that gravity ran sideways. High winds on big mountains trigger avalanches and rockfall and freeze hands and toes faster than you can beat a retreat. Accidents in paragliding (practiced by tens of thousands worldwide) usually occur from wing collapse as a result of wind shears. The cases are endless.

For brief spells, high winds might prove novel in an out-of-control kind of way. It's big adventure to paddle a sea kayak to shore from way out there when the winds start howling, but it's a desperate situation when you're stuck out there. As a rule, high wind adds such irritation and problems to most outdoor activities that's it usually better to go bowling.

When you're too far out to retreat, once the wind starts howling it's often best to hunker down. On land, find a windblock, like a boulder or rock face—or a cave if you're lucky—or anywhere that stuff is not raining down. Otherwise stay out in the open (and in the wind) to avoid windborne debris like flying tree limbs. Most winds swirl, so even while tucked into crannies and grottos, dust and dirt will blow around glasses and into your eyes. And forget the fire, for obvious reasons. The grief of battening down a campsite in high winds is good reason to seek a sheltered campsite and anchor it well in the first place. Be prepared to make some repairs, because you often will have to.

The grief of strong wind is known the second it stops, as if a thorn has been pulled from your soul. With proper protection (windproof hardshell coats and windshirts—wind whistles straight through mid-layer garments like pile), moderate winds are tolerable, even exciting if you don't have to perform. Adventure sports in medium to high winds are usually hellish. But it's part of the bargain for anything but short trips.

IT'S *NOT* PERSONAL

One time, way up on Middle Cathedral, huddled on a ledge as cold rain pounded down, I glared at my partner and old pro, Jim Bridwell—who hardly seemed bothered—and asked, "How can you just sit there and *like* this?!"

"It's not personal," is all he said. Later that summer I realized what Jim meant, because I had to—or coil my rope and quit.

What Bridwell had learned, and what he was modeling for me, was how to objectify my own experience. So long as I wanted a different world (sun and no rain), I was tortured by negative feelings, resented reality, and was prone to *reacting*. Shifting my attention away from regret and self-pity, I discovered a neutral position by *focusing entirely on the next indicated step*.

Look at video of the skier at the top of a downhill course; at the pro climber at the belay before a difficult lead; at a trekker before she heads across a 100-mile ice cap in howling wind. These people are not stuck in fear and doubts. They are locked in to the external world: objectifying, focusing, then taking the needed action. They momentarily have moved out of personal energy just as the ER doctor does when examining a broken leg. It's not personal. It's a job that needs doing.

Depersonalizing our experience is a tricky process to further explain, but we intuitively know it when we see it. The person acts like an adult, not a child ruled by fear and doubt. The key part to understand is that we learn to control our emotions not by trying to change or repress them (which only ramps up the pressure and self-doubts), but by externalizing our attention, objectifying, and focusing on solutions from a neutral perspective. When we check in with our feelings from this position, we are in a much better position to make decisions based on all factors.

So long as our attention is fused to our internal states, fear of risk and failure will paint the world in scary colors and direct us toward comfort and security. From an impersonal (neutral), objective mindset, we are clearer about the actual difficulties, and can act accordingly. When a coach or mentor understands this process and has students intentionally practice refining it, the skill is learned with greater ease and speed, and often at more depth.

Trying to be like Bridwell might have taken me a lifetime to ever get close. After I learned what he was doing and started practicing *that*, I was halfway there in a week.

Fine Tuning

It takes around 10,000 reps for a physical skill or activity to get neurologically grooved into our brainpans, and for the activity to become instinctive. So it goes with kayaking and surfing, mountain biking, or even long-distance hiking with a pack. After long layoffs, we must regain our base fitness, but once that's done, we don't have to learn so much as continuously make small adjustments relative to the game just ahead.

Interesting thing about muscle memory and old skills is that they only take us about 90 percent of the way home. That *last 10 percent* has to be worked at in a way that replicates the next challenge. What the hell does that mean? Professional ball sports have worked this out to a science.

Take a baseball player. Scouting reports say the next pitcher throws a lot of split-finger fastballs. So for the day before facing a pitcher offering that "stuff," that's what the pro practices. He or she already knows how to hit, but they benefit from facing a specific *kind* of pitch. That *last 10 percent* always deals with particulars.

It's a simple concept that carries over to every activity, and for the professional, it's standard practice as a project approaches, right up to game time. The goal is to blur the line between practice and the game. For the months before a hiker sets out to cross the Wind River Range in Wyoming, knowing she must slog over dozens of mountain passes, she starts putting in miles on hilly terrain so her practice flows into the project. If a surfer is heading to Hawaii with his sights on Pipeline, which involves powerful tube riding on a right breaking wave, he finds a similar wave to serve as a mock-up, and he practices on that.

The most important work happens just before game time. Go to an NBA game, and during half time watch what shots the players practice, right up to when the buzzer sounds for the second half. They'll take the same shots in the game, and the last second practice sharpens those shots. All of this seems dead obvious, yet few go this route. The reason was told in Harvey Penick's masterful book on golf.

When an amateur golfer asked Harvey (a renowned coach) how to most easily improve their game, he said, "Practice your short game." Since the majority of shots during a round of golf are chips and putts, your score is most easily lowered by practicing the strokes most commonly used. Except few wanted to do so. Instead they wanted to practice driving, where they could mash the ball and watch it sail. Way more fun. But it's no fun carding a 105 when a little practice could bring it down to 90.

You don't need to be a pro to practice like one. Not as hard or obsessively, but just as smart. While few ever bother, opting for more fun instead, those who practice smart wear the biggest smiles.

ICARUS SYNDROME

Sometime in the 1990s, extreme sports became a catchphrase applied to most any activity where risk and fear were sizable parts of the bargain. In some cases, like wingsuit skydiving, as wingsuiters kept going in and the death toll soared, risk become a grim endgame. The "Icarus Syndrome," as some called it, devoured scores of people who misjudged the margins by that much.

No matter the pursuit, people make names for themselves and forge careers by being the first to accomplish longstanding prizes and challenges that many have failed and sometimes died attempting: linking the veins of that river (underwater) cave, surfing the biggest wave, climbing the face of this mountain. Mountains, in particular, are where citizen adventurers can overreach themselves. Guides and the services they offer are a windfall to many.

However, on big, illustrious mountains at altitude, guided clients sometimes find themselves in a kind of military operation, laying siege to a colossal prize. The deaths-by-overcrowding on Everest bring this to light, when upward of 200 mountaineers get log-jammed on the summit ridge, far into the "death zone" (above 26,000 feet), and people start dropping left and right. When clients are marshaled up a mountain they could never manage on their own, mixed outcomes are expected. Getting guided to your death is a controversial issue we'll never resolve here. Point is, chasing prizes (the alpine version of trophy hunting) can blunt our mindfulness, reducing the adventure to a miserable death march.

Ambitious professionals are sometimes no better off. As adventure sports caught fire and the last great prizes continued falling, the only ones left for the aspiring ace were often so hard and so dangerous that the game split into two streams. Surfing provides a clear example of this.

Big wave surfing had been around since the early 1950s, but most surfers were fine with smaller, relatively safe waves where they performed increasingly impossible technical moves (inspired, in part, by aerial skateboarding tricks.). A big wave resurgence occurred in the early 1990s as more venues (beyond those found on the fabled North Shore of Hawaii) opened up, like Jaws, on

Maui, and Mavericks, in central California. For a moment, media attention shifted from the technical surfing found in contests and throughout "free" surfing, to a growing cast of people challenging waves of unheard-of heights—"Men who Ride Mountains," as the movie title suggests, though now women have very much joined the ride.

The tipping point happened in August 2000, at a Tahitian break called Teahupo'o, where Laird Hamilton is credited with surfing the "heaviest wave" ever ridden, documented in the film *Riding Giants*. When a photo of the ride appeared on the cover of *Surfer Magazine*, both the public and the surfing world were shocked to see Laird, looking like Ant Man, locked inside the streaming, three-story tube, peeling over a coral reef that would outright kill more than one surfer in the following years. This put some current and aspiring pros in a tough position.

"If this is what I have to do to be a professional surfer these days," one wrote, "forget it!" Over time, attention shifted back to technical surfing on survivable waves, because that's where all the numbers are. But a swelling sub-cult still pursued the biggest wave, till presently, at a break called Nazaré, in Portugal, people are bombing down combers reaching 80 feet high. And the swell goes on.

The same dynamic can be found in most every adventure sport. One stream, by far the largest, pursues absolute difficulty under relatively "safe" conditions, though using the word *safe* for any adventure can quickly backfire. A much smaller group, ignoring the old maxim to never pursue difficulty and risk at the same time (*If it's hard, it better be safe; if it's safe, go ahead and push it*), chases projects so extreme that success is unlikely unless everything goes perfectly—the weather and conditions, the teamwork, mustering the performances of a lifetime, all of which are hard to pull off individually, and almost impossible collectively. Doing so requires more luck than many have, and people continue to die by enchantment—enchanted by past successes, when all the stars aligned and they pulled off the miraculous. So they throw the dice again, knowing the house has the advantage.

At this most dangerous end of the game, the prize, though meaningful, is largely trumped by the high of enchantment, of drawing so close to the edge that eternity becomes a sensation. I went there myself, on occasion, so no one can accuse me of being smart. I have no explanation or excuses, or even a point to offer. In two days, when I have to attend another memorial for someone I loved and admired, I'll have no words, only a crooked smile for his many friends, his parents, and his wife, and will stand there in my Sunday pants and shirt feeling like the last man on earth. After half a life of making lifelong bonds in the wilderness, you never get used to that ritual of grief. Experts who draw close to the edge are well aware of the risks, but if we owe anything to the dead it's to keep those risks as talking points. Now, more than ever.

A few years ago, a line was crossed that cannot, perhaps, be nudged forward, beyond which even preternatural skill is not enough, a kill zone so hungry and unpredictable that nobody can survive there for long. Perhaps every generation believes they have reached that line, but the march never stops because younger, stronger, more ambitious men and women feel they can go further. Not surprisingly, some do, and the human limit is redefined once more. The vast majority of world-class performers are content to approach that line, pulling back near the edge, while a few, given to enchantment, rush toward the void. Others who've survived the spell of enchantment are stepping forward, at the risk of being hypocrites, offering cautionary tales. I don't expect people to listen. I never did. But it's hard to watch, and impossible to stay silent.

Things They Said

BROTHER GAINES

Bob Gaines came out of the 1970s So Cal sports system as a skilled long jumper and all-state running back, was nearly as thick as he was tall, had hair all over his body except on his head (by thirty he was bald as an egg), and from the day he first dropped in from Manhattan Beach and onto the grainy rock out at Joshua Tree National Park, was a relentless pioneer and kind of Mr. Chips to his many peers and the legions of climbers who followed.

Bob climbed "over a million" routes (including hundreds of first ascents) spanning a forty-year career and was a favorite topic of conversation, wild rumors, and droll slander that were sideways expressions of the love and admiration we all felt for Brother Gaines (he had dozens of nicknames). Wherever Bob went, he was The Man, showing a maturity and solidness that most of us lacked, and which made Bob an excellent guide and his Vertical Adventures climbing school one of the best in the country.

Part of our curiosity about Brother Gaines derived from his favored venue—slab climbing. Burley Bob belonged on strenuous cracks, not arty slabs, where finesse, balance, and deft movement are keys to the castle. Nonetheless, Bob became such a slab maestro that, according to the word on the trail, "even God couldn't explain it." He was like a freight train dancing and skipping on the track. Lynn Hill, many-time World Cup sport climbing champion, said it looked like Bob and the slab were dating. Others witnessed Bald Bob on the bald faces and said he deserved his own bobble head doll, that Brother Gaines was the Brother Gaines of slab climbing, and so forth.

Over time it became a thing to deliver random asides about Bob, out of the blue and sans context. We might be eating breakfast, changing a tire, or toughing out a marathon drive when someone would say, 'How does one acquire such top-drawer polish as Brother Gaines?' I'll never be that cool in my life, someone else would offer. The game was on from there. Bob was one of the most prolific climbers in America, but his CV was nothing compared to his legend in popular lore. In the tightest of jams, we'd sometimes ask: What would Brother Gaines do? He gave even the best of us someone to live up to.

Of the many things said about Brother Gaines, one stands out, from back when Bob had a beard and was at the top of his game, circa 2000. A dozen of us were huddled around a campfire up in County Park, close by Tahquitz Rock, when the booze was gone, heads were starting to nod, and all eyes were staring at the fire.

"I hate it when people compare Brother Gaines to Jesus," said my friend David Katz. "I mean, he's great and all, but he's not Brother Gaines."

FUNKY?

The evolution of sea kayaking is an interesting study full of colorful characters pulling off adventures all the more remarkable because many are so little known. At the top of the list is Ed Gillet's 1987, 2,200-mile, sixty-four-day epic kayak paddle (solo and unsponsored) from Monterey, California, to Maui, Hawaii, "an impossible idea that would spin the paddling world off its axis," according to *Canoe & Kayak Magazine*. Many still consider Gillet's Pacific Ocean crossing the greatest paddling feat of them all, right there with the greatest solo adventures in modern history.

When the news first broke about Ed's adventure, it stoked the embers of those already steeped in water sports, from Olympic flatwater kayakers and canoeists, to outrigger paddlers, to those competing in the Bud-Light surf-ski comps during summer weekends, to people like DB and I who grew up close to the beach and crossed over from other adventure sports. This group was performance oriented and wanted to be like Ed Gillet, though to a far lesser degree. A much larger crowd were "day-trippers," inspired by Ed's heroics and drawn toward basic participation. Few had designs on big adventures, or even paddling the 26 miles of open ocean from the So Cal coast over to Catalina Island.

For a casual fitness paddler, performance was usually trumped by safety, so slower, stable kayaks were favored. Performers needed something that flew across the water, since covering mileage was much of the game. This group went with surf-ski-inspired crafts, with a narrow width and hull shape, a long waterline and plumb, and a high-volume bow, features best suited for long-distance journeys since they tracked well on both flatwater and in rolling swell. The basic shape was roughly 20 feet long and wide as your hips, and the best models looked and moved like heat-seeking missiles. Tippy, yes, so they took some getting used to.

The numbers paddling performance kayaks in open ocean were never many, so those who did naturally fell into informal groups, with lots of intermingling since we often carpooled to the other group's water to, say, paddle en masse out to the Santa Cruz Islands, 30 miles off the Ventura coastline. In our little group, drawn mostly from the local lifeguard crew, great care and consideration was given to the paint jobs we'd apply to our boats. Inspired by late 1990s funk, every design was appraised on its funk factor. Some paddlers went with drip-and-sling styles à la Jackson Pollack. Various day-glow mixtures also caught on. Gauche combos of Scottish plaid and African Kitenge were common. Then Mort Stein painted his boat gold pearl (Mort looked like he was paddling a gold bar across the sea), and things went postal from there.

Flames, camo, paisley, polka dot, and every imaginable combination was busted out for group approval and to "indemnify funk." The grand arbiter of our creations was Jimmy Hines, who had an unrivaled collection of classic Motown tracks and worked at the Getty Museum (gardener), so could render his judgments with authority. But when Jill Lopez showed up down in Zuma Beach with her boat painted exactly like an argyle sock (accents in lime and hot pink), we could only stand and stare at such majesty. That included Jimmy Hines as well, who only shook his head.

"Well," asked Jill, grinning at Jimmy. "Is it funky?"

"Is it funky?" asked Jimmy. "That's James Brown in a Caddy lowrider full of blue cheese funky!"

Like so many groups of adventure junkies in so many places spread over the decades, our informal little group of sea kayakers rode life's currents in various directions till the people and their crazy boats remain only in dreams and a few dog-eared photos. But every so often I think of Jill Lopez's pink and lime argyle kayak, and hope it's still around somewhere. It belongs in the Smithsonian, as an avatar of twentieth-century funk.

OUT BEYOND THE AUBADE

If we get up at day break and write a poem it's called an aubade. Black marks on white paper, a secret code about who we are at the crack of dawn. If we get up with the sun and ride a wave on a board there's no secret and no marks left on the water. Sometimes we find what a poem can never know, when we drag out of bed all thick headed and beat down to the sand, pull on a slimy sandy wet suit and paddle out, still dazed by dreams, two half-closed eyes, prisms of a thousand colors shifting, the yellows shining out bright and clear as the sea blues into view just below, now melting into green as we carve towards the big orange sun. Out beyond the aubade.

—Written on the back of an oversized postcard my friend Dean Helms sent me from Fiji, with a photo ("Sunrise over Teahupo'o") of the legendary surf spot on the front.

Great Wave

Joe was a student of mine in a writer's symposium. He showed
promise but kept cranking out stiff, formal-register junk reflecting
none of his natural voice, passion, or personality. One of the other
instructors suggested that he recall something personal, something
that had stayed with him, deep in his bones, and to spontaneously
write it out, without analyzing or trying to sound like a writer. Joe
tucked himself into a little corner of the library. That afternoon he
read this to the class:

> Duke Kahanamoku was Olympic swimming champion and a
> legendary surfer who Sal and I learned about during junior
> high at Pacific Beach in San Diego. Our home room teacher
> was a surfer like us and he had a Xerox copy of the Surfer
> Magazine with Duke's last interview, with pictures of the
> Hawaiian with the gold medal and standing next to his fifteen
> foot koawood longboard. And another shot of the champion as
> an old man, walking in the sand out by Diamond Head. Sal
> Xeroxed the Xeroxed copy and in a few weeks we could recite
> parts of that interview almost word for word, especially the bit
> about the famous wave at Waikiki, which the Duke rode for
> over a mile before kicking out. "A ride for the ages." Toward the
> end the Duke talked about another great wave he knew was
> waiting for him, and how some day he was going to get it. "But
> this time I'm not kicking out," he said. "I'll just keep on going."
> This part wasn't so exciting so we only read it once. The Duke
> was seventy-seven years old when he did that interview, and
> Sal was twenty-three when doctors told him he had a month
> to live. It was awful to watch, and I didn't have a clue. Then
> right at the end I dug out the old Xeroxed copy of Surfer and I
> read the interview to Sal one last time. I went over the last bit
> twice, the part we always skipped before. By then Sal couldn't
> even talk but he knew exactly what he was hearing and he
> never struggled after that. His girlfriend couldn't explain it.
> She didn't know the Duke had been our hero since we were

fourteen, and that all along he'd been waiting for that great wave, and for Sal, because the Duke never liked to surf alone. Now he wouldn't have to. He just reached back and pulled Sal onto a perfect blue curl on a perfect blue day. And they didn't kick out, either. Not this time. They just kept on going.

We Walk the Coast Together

Several years ago I was asked to write a one-paragraph introduction for a photo book (mostly by celebrated art photogs) on beach culture. The book never got published, but I still have a copy of the intro:

Eon after eon the waves wash up and retreat in a thin white veil, pin holes bubbling in the beach. Half a mile inland, the seconds grind our minds flat as we turn in a circle, squinting from the glare, tiny arms raised, amazed and terrified to be made alive. We hook up. We rock life, silently holding our breath, trying to duck-dive the close-out. Sometimes I am vexed by boredom but life happens quickly. I barely got the van unloaded and already I'm too old, she's too hip, he's too drunk, and you, dear friend, have too many damn tattoos. We are different people. And in other places, as the years harden between us, this might make us strangers. But here, at the edge of the sea, we walk the coast together. All we ask of the running tide is the chance to return. Where the water meets the sand.

Herb

My friend Herb was born into the biking world, starting with his grade school days riding BMX, then on to mountain biking and most anything else on two wheels. Though never much of a competitor, Herb was so immersed in biking that the marketing director for a leading bike manufacturer swore Herb shaved with chain lube. Herb was always dragging me along to biking events, and I was never sure if the biking or his laconic commentary was the reason I always joined him.

One time after watching Austrian mountain biker Valentina Holl flow like water down a challenging run, Herb said, "She lays her bike on that track like Hans Zimmer lays music on film." Said Herb to the Giant rep after test-driving a new carbon fiber, full-suspension mountain bike: "This rig's so tight I had to loosen my belt to ride it."

Herb called in a few favors and snagged us front row seats for the BMX Big Air comp at the X Games, one of the wildest stadium events in creation. After an electrifying semifinals, Herb said, "Gets any crazier out here it'll violate several articles of the Geneva Convention."

And toward the end of a weekday run down Sullivan Canyon, which follows a pedestrian singletrack through a green gulch in the Santa Monica Mountains, Herb pulled over at the last stream crossing, smiled, and said, "My Monday just got a lot less Monday."

DRIVEN BY PHANTOMS

While waiting for a table at the Rose Cafe in Venice, California, I noticed a couple big framed photos hanging on the wall. One showed several windsurfers on a winter wave close by the Venice pier. The caption read:

How strange and how fantastic that a wave is an invisible energy source moving through the transparent medium of water. And no one has ever seen the wind. So in a sense, all we see here is the harvest of the unseen, and the people who harness these hidden forces are in fact ghost riders, driven by phantoms.

WHAT RELIGION?

The show was airing on CBS so they had the money but didn't want to spend it on a helicopter mount. That left me to try to grab some usable footage by lashing myself to a strut inside the chopper and hanging out the side door, hand-holding a 16mm film camera. This rarely works, especially over the Grand Canyon, where grand winds start gusting once the sun is low and the light is just right, and it didn't work now. So we drove to several scenic turnouts, chasing the light, and I tried to nail a few master scenics that could do justice to 1.9 billion years of geological history and one hell of a gulch.

Dusk fell and we started packing up. We'd been so pressed for time I'd barely seen the canyon, except through the viewfinder. Finally we had a moment and gazed down into The Grand as shadows filled the space. I looked at my camera assistant, Don, from Macon, Georgia, and asked, "What do you think?" After a long, silent gander, Don said, "What religion is that, anyhow?"

CRACK IN HALF

Ted moved from Santa Monica to Long Beach, half an hour down the 405 freeway, to get closer to his girlfriend. Then the girlfriend went away but Ted stayed. The traffic was so bad during waking hours that I kept putting off driving down for a visit till Ted wouldn't accept 'No.' He'd recently bought two stand-up paddleboards off Craig's List and swore that stroking around the local marina was well worth the drive.

I didn't get to Ted's house till late afternoon and the sky was all purple and orange when we starting paddling Ted's new boards out across the water. After half a mile we tucked into a protected inlet. The wind died and the water, still as a millpond, was a fiery palette of pastels. The boards jumped gently with our strokes, and the glide between only got two stars because it didn't last forever. Somewhere a seagull cawed. I had the feeling that we weren't flowing across the water, rather we'd found a still point and the world was flowing around us. If we weren't in the Golden City, we were in the neighborhood.

"If this was any cooler," said Ted, "I'd crack in half and come back as a parrot."

Still not sure what he meant by that, but you get the idea.

HOUSE BAND FOR HELL

DB grew up with money but absentee parents, and Desert Sun High School, up in Idyllwild, California, is where DB and one hundred other rich kids were shipped off to boarding school. Since Desert Sun was close by Suicide Rock, the kids with energy and restless dreams found their way to the cliffside, and that's where I met DB. We were both seventeen. Over the following decades we'd go jungleering in New Guinea, caving in Venezuela, climbing all over, and ended up in places not found on any map. DB later got his PhD in literature from the University of Irvine after stints at several ivy league institutions. But it was early on, before Spencer, Raleigh, and all the rest had their way with him that DB spontaneously delivered some of the finest deadpan lines I've ever heard spoken in, or about, The Remote.

Like the time we were hiking to some new cliff above Ojai, California, and a flock of songbirds chimed in with such a funky refrain one of us stopped and said, "What *is* that?" And DB said, "That's what makes the birds bobble their heads when they walk."

Another time, in the jungle, don't remember where, the mosquitoes were eating us alive, the rain fell in an annoying drizzle, and the cicadas, birds, monkeys, and all their friends were making such a racket one us lost his mind and screamed up at the enclosing canopy, "Shut the fuck up!"

"Ain't no use," said DB. "That's the house band for hell . . . and we're in it."

Over on Oahu, Hawaii, we were bodysurfing at a popular break in rare conditions—good-sized waves, with no wind and a glass smooth sea. You'd kick into a comber, plunge down the face in a partial free fall then glide out the shoulder as if nestled in velvet. Another of our friends showed up just as we were finishing our first session and asked, "How is it?"

"It's like being rolled in the greatest cashmere blanket ever invented," said DB, "and getting thrown off a bridge into a river of smoothness."

SO MUCH WONDERFUL

The drive up from Fresno to Yosemite follows 32 miles of winding road. An open view of the valley is masked by hills and arroyos till you rumble through a half-mile-long tunnel ending at the top of a bluff. Then the road pitches down the incline to the floor of the valley. Just past the tunnel and off the road is Tunnel Overlook, a two-acre parking lot running to a low guardrail beyond which is a vista for the ages, sighting straight down the mile-wide valley with waterfalls cascading and El Capitan rearing and meadows fanning and rivers meandering and, far in the distance, the black-streaked face of Half Dome, lording over it all like Father Time.

No matter the month or the weather, Tunnel Overlook is usually jammed with cars and tour buses and swarming with people taking pictures and soaking in the view. This was the situation when I was biking in from Yosemite West, a dozen or so miles away, and wheeled up to the guardrail and stopped next to a pack of bikers who'd just motored in from Sacramento. One of them looked over and asked, "You a local," and I said, "When I'm here I am."

He chuckled, gazed out over the valley, and asked, "How'd they ever fit so much wonderful into such a narrow valley?"

THE SPIRE

America's first big technical rock climb was Bestor Robinson, Dick Leonard, and Jules Eichorn's 1934 ascent of Higher Cathedral Spire (Yosemite Valley), which at 1,320 feet from base to crown, was North America's largest freestanding pinnacle. Ever since, this route has remained an iconic, must-do climb and a classic among classics. For many years there was an old ammo can/register stashed in the rocks on the summit, with a loose-leaf notebook (and other mementos) where people signed their name and scribbled out their thoughts. I took photos of some of the pages.

That final pitch! wrote Jenifer B. Makes me wanna do cartwheels. Jeepers! said Randy U. This ain't meant for mortal man.

This Spire confirms the existence of Heaven, wrote Brett N, or proves the divinity of Nature or expresses ultimate beauty or some damn thing. Thank you for the heights of where this climb took us. Just what my soul was looking for.

Forget It!

Who can forget the photos of Doug Scott crawling off Ogre I (Karakoram Range, Pakistan) in heavy weather, one of the greatest survival stories of them all?

Doug Scott . . . make that *Sir* Doug Scott, now that he's been knighted. I was a reckless teenager when I first met Doug in Yosemite and we tried to cross the Merced to climb the Rostrum. Except the river was flooding and we couldn't clear the current, hopping rock to rock, like I'd promised. Finally I said, "To hell with it. I'm roping up and swimming across."

Doug laughed and said, "Forget it. You'll drown." Doug was older and looked like Moses with his beard, plus he'd just bagged a new route on Everest and had that clout. So I forgot it and we hitched over to The Cookie and climbed *Meat Grinder*.

I sometimes wonder about Sir Doug, who after our encounter in Yosemite forged on to Kanchenjunga, Nuptse, and a dozen other peaks. How did he survive all that? He must have had better sense. Or maybe he knew that an ogre unchained was a cannibal, and also knew that I didn't. So he said, "Forget it. You'll drown." Makes me want to fly over to England and thank the knight who saved my ass, and later crawled off the Ogre on two broken legs.

I Know that Stream Is Close

In his book, *Biophilia* (1984), biologist Edward O. Wilson declared that humans possess an innate love of nature. Wilson's argument was persuasive, said the *Times*, yet "it sounds at best like an aspiration dressed up as a hypothesis, at worst like woolly-headed romanticism."

In the generation since, journalist Richard Louv coined the phrase "Nature-Deficit Disorder" to describe the growing disconnection between people and nature. Around the same time, research in Japan found that immersing yourself in the natural world significantly reduces stress and wards off depression. In response, Japan's Forestry Agency created a network of "Forest Therapy" trails on which rangers monitor visitors' blood pressure (in order to "objectify" the results). This and other forms of ecotherapy (aka, nature therapy or green therapy) all sang the same refrain: "The more nature, the better you feel."

All of this fed the emergent field of ecopsychology, "which stems from the belief that people are part of the web of life and that our psyches are not isolated or separate from our environment." What's telling in that last quote is the word *belief*, as though our place in the natural order of things is moot, that we no longer share a connection to the larger community of life, but there's little confusion over how this came about.

The cultures we built required harmonizing our instincts within the larger tribe, focused as it was on comfort, security, and thought. As civilization advanced, indigenous people were trampled underfoot and The Remote became the chaos we "transcended," though we still lived on the face of the earth. Then the cyber world cut the connection altogether. When the Academy Award–winning documentary *Free Solo* (chronicling climber Alex Honnold's ropeless ascent of 3,000-foot-high El Capitan, in Yosemite Valley) basically hard-wired viewers back into the wild places, the sudden reconnect was so jarring that many could explain the drama only in terms of fear. What was the point? some wondered. But millions went, nevertheless, pushed by unseen hands.

Viewers and critics agreed that *Free Solo* transcended sport by a mile, and that its allure and gravity derived from a real person facing a real-world challenge with real stakes. Psychologists warn that the shocking rise in suicide rates are in some way linked to ersatz cyber worlds confounding our need and connection to real people and natural things. Many of our heroes are not even human anymore. They're CGI phonies with no skin in the game. The various forms of ecotherapy are simple reminders that we evolved as a species in response to living in the wilds, meaning our very brains are inexorably linked to natural surroundings.

We were largely fashioned by ancient rhythms, with a set of common needs, desires and physical norms that far outweigh our differences. The "Call of the Wild" still stirs within us, if only as a whisper. Not surprisingly, some are discovering that the wild places help allay the fragmentation and disconnect that we often feel in the "real world." But there's something deeper at play here.

Like the time I was mountain biking the challenging (to me) trails spilling off the mountains behind Santa Barbara, California. The last stretch followed a rutty dirt path flanking a quiet little stream draped with elms and ferns. Just before a short rise and the road, I came across an old man hobbling down the path and carrying a small oxygen bottle feeding a plastic breather fastened to his nose. Whatever ailed the old man, it had him for keeps. He looked slightly disoriented, and I wondered if he hadn't wandered off from wherever and was lost.

No. He wasn't lost. He was looking for the stream. He still had all his marbles, he said, "and I know that stream is close." His eyes seemed to flash, like a pilgrim on the Hajj, returning to Mecca, or a place not found "in the comfort and privacy of our own homes."

FISH STORIES

One of the boons of the wild places are the marvelous "fish stories" that wildly embellish the people, places, and things folks claim to have encountered outdoors. These are simple entertainments, intentionally absurd, and have been treasured by mankind since the First Caveman, standing around the campfire, looked at his people and said, "No shit. There I was . . ." No outdoor education is complete without a few classic fish stories. Here's one of my favorites.

The Integratron (situated half a dozen miles south of Joshua Tree National Park, in the high desert of Southern California) is a 38-foot-high, 55-foot-diameter rejuvenation and time machine based on the design of Moses' Tabernacle, the writings of Nikola Tesla, and telepathic directions from extraterrestrials. The magnificent, all-wooden dome, completed in 1959, was the brainchild of the late George Van Tassel, erstwhile host of the annual Giant Rock Spacecraft Convention and author of *The Council of Seven Lights*. Quoting Van Tassel, the entire area "is sited on a powerful geomagnetic vortex, making it the third most cosmic place on earth."

Today, the Integratron is the only all-wood, acoustically perfect sound chamber in the United States. That might not sound like much, but the structure is magnificent, a real work of art, and all done with wooden dowels and glue and so forth. A labor of love with a few little green men tossed in for flavor.

One day when flash floods washed them out of the popular climbing spots in the park, my friends Hans and Jimmy drove to the Integratron for a look-see. The moment they found the place, in forgotten desert out past Yucca Valley, and took the tour and heard about extraterrestrials and time machines, a whopper started taking shape.

The way Hans tells it, Gus the tour guide said the Integratron was missing a key part so the time traveling capacities were never tested before Van Tassel went and died, but just a week before, Van Tassel's granddaughter found the missing part in her mother's attic (Scarlet Van Tassel, George's widow, had recently passed away). Gus described the mysterious part as a kind of octagon/geodesic-shaped widget, also wooden, slightly larger than a soccer ball, and fitted with a fantastic articulation of small oak gears and do-dads and several windows and other stuff. Van Tassel's notes indicated the "Vortex Catalyst" could harness and direct the robust cosmic energies pulsing from the geomagnetic vortices on which the Integraton was built.

After the tour broke up and the others left, Jimmy grilled Gus about the Vortex Catalyst and learned to his and Hans's amazement that nobody had yet stuck the widget into the hole in the floor designed for that purpose. "Fetch the widget and jam it home," said Jimmy, a born fool, but anxious to see, after half a century, if the Integratron was real or baloney.

So Gus fetches the widget and keys it into the hole, and the structure pulsed and hummed, but subtly, according to Hans. There was a wicker chair dead center, below a conspicuous hole in the ceiling, and Jimmy instructed Hans to sit down in the chair, and he said, "Bite me." So Gus set Floyd, the widow Scarlet Van Tassel's beagle, in the chair. It sits there for a moment. Then its ears perk up and suddenly the beagle is gone. One second the boys are looking right at it, not 10 feet away. And the next moment, Floyd is simply not there at all. Vanished.

Ten minutes later, Gus gets a call from a hiker out at the park, 25 miles away, who was trekking through the desert by a remote rock tower called "Lost Pencil," when he came across the raptured beagle, wandering in wide circles and covered in a funky marmalade, but otherwise fine. The hiker had apparently called the number on the dog collar.

What I've Learned

For many years, *Rock & Ice* magazine has periodically run a column called "What I've Learned," featuring many of the top people in the sport, who told their stories in a series of short paragraphs. Here are a few (abridged) of my favorites:

"When I started climbing, I fell in love with it. The climbing, the travel, the adventure, living outside, doing everything outside. It was the first thing that made sense to me.

"What I've learned from traveling is not about climbing. It's about how you experience the world *through* climbing. Like when people say Muslims hate women, I say, "Oh, really? I was treated with respect.

"I don't want to get my experience from *Time* magazine and CNN. I want to see how people live. The kindness I've been shown—people will give you their last date and last water. I've been treated with such kindness around the world, it makes me want to be a better person."

—Brittany Griffith

"The minute you ever think you know where you're going in life you're almost certain to be disabused. In some ways I wish I'd never had the accident in Peru and I'd managed to achieve what I'd hoped for in climbing, and I never did. So that's a regret, but in a strange way the experience was almost a privilege. Out of it came lots of positive things. I would never have become a writer if I hadn't ended up in that bloody crevasse."

—Joe Simpson

"When I look back on every big adventure, I can identify one pivotal moment that would either lead to us finishing, or not. Now I can recognize this moment while I'm in it. That's been invaluable because I know when to push, when to dig a bit deeper. I try not to stop until something external stops me."

—Steve House

"I had mastered misery. So I was well-suited for the last two decades of losing balance, coordination and sense of touch, contorting hands and drop foot. Gradual loss of strength. Whole-body spasms as painful as anything I've ever known. Gastrointestinal tract shutting down. Struggling hours each day to clear phlegm and fluids from lungs. Weakened from atrophying diaphragm muscles. The agony of trying to communicate with paralyzed vocal chords. Unable to reach my granddaughter with more than a hug and a kiss.

"Climbing on the Eiger, I met my true self, at the deepest level. I discovered that who I am is enough. That I could go back to my life and do my best, and it would be O.K. That I could be a better father than I had been in the past, and be there for Sonja as she grew up. That my love for her was more important than my mistakes. I saw a way through turmoil then, just as I see a way through each day's challenges now.

"I learned in those moments that all of life is really about learning."

—Jeff Lowe (basically invented modern American alpinism. Jeff suffered from a neurological disease similar to ALS for approximately eighteen years. He died on August 24, 2018, surrounded by his daughter, Sonja, as well as cousin, George Lowe, and close friends.)

"I've learned that when you make a mistake it's usually not the first mistake that kills you. It's rushing into something else trying to recover from the first one.

"I've learned that on a big trip you go with equal partners, which means everyone has an equal opportunity and responsibility for decision-making. It's important to be aware on a big adventure when anyone, including me, is too intimidated or exhausted to collaborate and contribute equally. If I sense that this is happening, we all immediately go down."

—Steve Swenson

"Things don't stay the same long enough to make plans. So I don't base any decisions on guesses about the future. What I'm doing now is what I'm doing, and it always leads me to the next thing. For me the biggest goal is evolution.

"I always have a list of dream adventures, and no matter how much I do, the list never gets shorter."

—Steph Davis

Nature Writing

Due west, the anvil-flat Central Valley, which dominates the geo-graphical center of California, stretched out and swept off the edge of the world. This was our first day on the climb, and the adventure felt as huge as my faith and ambition. I was too green for soul searching, was clueless about inner demons, and I wasn't trying to kick heroin. I loved adventure sports and the rush of high places.

We were bivouacked on a small ledge, 800 feet up the sheer granite face of The Watchtower, in Kings Canyon National Park. As we ate tuna out of a can, sipped water, and settled in for the night, the empty distances of the Central Valley commanded my attention. I couldn't look away, though the open vista, graying into night, looked glum and unremarkable. Subtly at first, I got the sinking feeling that there was nothing out there. Or rather, all that I saw was fleeting, was written in rain. I knew, as a concept, that nothing lasts, all things change, and someday I would die. But when the concept became my lived experience, my sense of permanence, of existing across time, dissolved in midair. In one turn of the screw, the things I took as substantial, including myself and the mountain we were on, became so many bubbles geysering from a void.

This feeling kindled a bizarre, bewildering state more easily imagined than described. Goethe said that he wanted to perceive "whatever holds the world together in its inmost folds." Back then I couldn't have formulated such a question. I only wanted to get to the top of The Watchtower. Then my world came apart at the seams. Impossibly, the arrangement of things had somehow inverted. Concrete reality had fallen out, leaving only foam in a vacuum, and a felt sense of living death.

With nothing to hold on to, I somehow managed to summit the wall and stumble back home. For several weeks I wandered in a zombie state, sleeping like a wild animal, on and off or not at all. Why climb or do anything when the whole shebang was a dead-end kabuki? I tried everything imaginable to melt the chilling brain freeze of that state, which bent everything in its direction. Running. Lifting weights. Swimming in the ocean. A sweat lodge. Hard liquor. Nothing could so much as dent that state. Only slowly did I return to the world of solid objects.

I stuffed the experience for a decade, until I read a blurb by Jungian psychologist Robert Johnson, who, citing the myth of the Fisher King, said that most every young man naively blunders into the Grail Castle long before he can handle it. It's simply too big and too hot, so he runs for his life, not knowing where he's been. But the encounter never leaves him entirely, said Johnson. It forces a shift in consciousness he can neither live with nor entirely drop. That felt like a reach, dragging the Fisher King onto my ledge. Either way, the molten core of that state, and the anxious days that followed, were still too hot to unpack.

I never told a soul about my encounter on The Watchtower because there was no way I could coherently describe, much less explain, any of it. I must have read one hundred books and articles on altered states, meltdowns, and weird experiences but found nothing that captured the corrosive power of that state. My experience, I figured, was an outlier because so was I. A person not drawn to such extremes, who respected their own fear, could have gotten the message, whatever it was, in subtler doses. Only when something consumed me did it get my full attention and regard. Resolving that state eventually became a mission.

I made little progress. I started ranging through ancient wisdom texts like the Upanishads, the Buddhist Sutras, the Vedas, the

Zohar. I toughed out meditation retreats, half the time squirming on my cushion, ready to implode. Eventually I began to unwind from the middle and continued plowing through the old texts, which were so figurative and freighted with cultural mythology they felt maddeningly vague and ungraspable, but they all converged on two basic themes: impermanence and emptiness. Getting hold of either felt like shoveling smoke.

Then an old nun at a Zen retreat told me that impermanence and emptiness were not so much concepts but direct experiences that informed us about existence. The experiences, she said, usually deepened over time, as did our understanding that all forms are temporary, and that the whole shebang is empty, a confounding term for a bubbling void.

"What happens if you got the full dose of both, all at once?" I asked. "You wouldn't want that to happen," she said, "because at first they feel like death."

I felt the ground shift to quicksand so I backed off, later wondering about the old maxim that the poison is the medicine. What if that shattering state was just a dark moat surrounding the castle? With nothing to lose, I started searching out any open landscape and pocket of silence that evoked the penumbra of that state—on El Capitan, in the heart of the Venezuelan rain forest, in Zendos, on the frozen plane of the North Pole. I was never sure what I expected to happen. Everything felt nonlinear and random.

With nothing yet resolved, I bought a sack full of dog-eared anthologies on nature writing from Rustic Deity Used Books in Ontario, California. My curiosity with nature writing was unrelated to my experience on The Watchtower. I just wanted to see what others had written about my home turf. Though a recognizable and distinct tradition in English prose, which had existed for over 200 years, I knew little to nothing about the genre. The bag gathered dust in my closet till well after college, when I read a passage from Ralph Waldo Emerson in a magazine.

Not a form so grotesque, so savage, nor so beautiful but is an expression of some inherent quality in man the observer—an occult relation between the very scorpions and man. I feel the centipede in me—caiman, carp, eagle, and fox. I am moved by strange sympathies.

Whatever Emerson meant by these words, they intrigued me enough to fetch the bag of anthologies and wander in. It's telling to review the passages that I earmarked with a yellow highlighter, the first from *Anima Poetae*, an unpublished notebook (circa 1815) by Samuel Taylor Coleridge:

I have read of two rivers, the Rhone and the Adar, passing through Lake Geneva, yet all the while preserving their streams visibly distinct. In a far finer distinction, yet in a subtler union, are the streams of knowing and being. The lake is formed by the two streams in man and Nature as it exists in and for man; and up this lake we sail on the junction-line of the constituent streams, still pushing upward and sounding as we go, toward the common fountainhead of both, the mysterious source whose being is knowledge, whose knowledge is being—the adorable I AM IN THAT I AM.

The constituent streams had in this case flowed from the man described in *Confessions of an English Opium Eater*, and they sounded like it, but I took Coleridge's advice to push upward, skimming a century's worth of work to the next highlighted bit, from *The Outermost House* (1928), by Henry Beston.

Our fantastic civilization has fallen out of touch with the many aspects of nature, and with none more completely than with night. With lights and ever more lights, we drive the holiness and beauty of night back to the forests and the sea; the little villages, the crossroads even, will have none of it. Are modern folk afraid of night . . . that vast serenity, the mystery of space, the austerity of stars? Today's civilization is full of

people who have never even seen night. Yet to know only arti-
ficial night is as absurd and evil as to know only artificial day.

Maybe twenty-seven or twenty-eight at the time, and well
into adventuring, I'd come to appreciate Beston's point, how so
many people had lost touch with The Remote, whose paradoxical
windfalls I kept finding on my own, and throughout the nature
anthologies. Both ran counter to the pastoral bliss many imagine
from a distance. The moments that tempered and enriched often
sparked fear and doubts and a looming unknown that threatened
to swallow us whole.

This point was illustrated in a piece by John Burroughs, friend
and advocate of Walt Whitman, and one of the most popular
nature writers of the late nineteenth century. Burroughs joined
forces with Theodore Roosevelt and others in a war against "nature
fakers"—writers whose stories were full of talking rabbits and
mawkish jive, not at all what Burroughs found in the bowls of
Mammoth Cave, which is Henry Beston's "night" times a hundred. Wrote Burroughs:

> *The voice goes forth in these colossal chambers like a bird. When*
> *no word is spoken, the silence is of a kind never experienced on*
> *the surface of the earth, it is so profound and abysmal. This,*
> *and the absolute darkness, make a person with eyes feel as*
> *if he were face to face with the primordial nothingness. The*
> *objective universe is gone; only the subjective remains; the*
> *sense of hearing is inverted, and reports only the murmurs*
> *from within. The body feels the presence of unusual conditions*
> *through every pore.*

This was the first passage I had read anywhere by anybody that
had the imagery and high voltage of the state that had fried my
circuits. It only got better as Burroughs continued.

> *My thoughts took a decidedly sepulchral turn; I thought of my*
> *dead and of all the dead of the earth, and said to myself, the*

darkness and the silence of my last resting place is like this; to this we must all come at last. No vicissitudes of earth, no changes of season, nor sound of storm or thunder penetrate here; it is all one; a world beyond the reach of change, because beyond the reach of life. What peace, what repose, what desolation!

This familiar experience I found seconded in many other entries, summed up by Mary Austin in *The Land of Little Rain* (1903), writing about Death Valley, "the core of desolation," and how "one falls into the tragic key in writing about desert-ness."

That desert-ness had left me feeling like a tribe of one, so it felt encouraging to find others who had experienced the vast lonesomeness and had fallen into the rabbit hole. Over the years, as I worked through the anthologies as well as newer works, I saw that for all their varied tone and expression, the nature writers were of one voice about our mortality leaping off a backdrop of stillness, silence, and darkness, whenever encountered raw. I stuck with my counter-phobic pledge to seek out that backdrop and linger there, which sometimes felt like getting airmailed into space. The exercise went against reason and instinct and seemed, at crux moments, like approaching a black hole—the pendulum of time fell off and rather than soar, I was stopped cold, frozen by silence, as Burroughs went on to describe, per his encounter in Mammoth Cave.

At a point in one of the great avenues, if you stop and listen, you hear a slow, solemn ticking like a great clock in a deserted hall; you hear the slight echo as it fathoms and sets off the silence. It is called the clock, and is caused by a single large drop of water falling every second into a little pool. A ghostly kind of clock there in the darkness, that is never wound up and that never runs down. It seems like a mockery where time is not, and change does not come—the clock of the dead.

But a clock nonetheless. Not time itself, the chameleon of science, but an echo sufficiently loud to suggest intervals, duration, a chain of moments divided by a drop. To remain in this slow cascade was to crawl back onto that ledge on The Watchtower, which felt like tempting the Devil. Every part of me screamed out to run for the light and sounds and living things. Problem was, as Robert Johnson promised, I'd had a shift in consciousness I could neither live with nor entirely drop. All I could do was try to hold my ground. Unnerving at times, for sure, but the tornado had an eye.

In my mounting experiences in high places, from Canada to Baja, Mexico, I'd come to know, respect, and dangle in awe at the psychological gravity found a half mile off the ground—the sucking void, and the vast open reaches in what's known to many climbers as the Big Empty. It's no wonder that void, within and without, is so well represented, and sometimes idealized, in nature writing, but this is strong medicine, and the cheer dies fast when the desolation reaches a magnitude we can no longer scale. As the nun said, "You don't want that to happen." But it had, and a resolution, one as deeply felt as that state, still escaped me.

Any possible link between my experience on The Watchtower and the rarefied writings of the nature writers was something I questioned from the start. What Beston, Burroughs, Austin, and others had experienced—in caves, deserts, and silent nights—sounded pensive and morose, but it didn't feel shattering. It didn't feel like it destroyed their innate trust in the surety of things. It didn't feel like it atomized their self. I placed no virtue on that experience, and never imagined it gave me privileged knowledge, but it did make me keep searching for others who'd been hurled so far off their axis that the memory still haunted years later. Maybe they'd found some meaning or insight so far lost on me. Robert Johnson had mentioned a castle, but what was in it?

As I journeyed deeper into nature writing, I finally found a handful of others who, with uncanny accuracy, described something of my own experience by way of the stillness, solitude, and unremitting bleakness they found in the Patagonia wastelands, traditionally called The End of the Earth. As portrayed by

Argentine-born British writer, W. H. Hudson, in *Afoot in England,* the Big Empty:

> *. . . shadows forth the heartless voids and immensities of the universe, then stabs us from behind with the thought of annihilation. We are let all at once into the true meaning of those disquieting and seemingly indefinable emotions so often experienced, even by the most ardent loves of nature and solitude, in uninhabited deserts, on great mountains, and on the sea.*

While that first blush is the terror of extinction, I wondered if hardier souls than Hudson or myself, folks grounded in the natural sciences, might provide a cooler take on the same terrain. Consider this passage from Charles Darwin's classic *Voyage of H.M.S. Beagle*:

> *I find that the plains of Patagonia frequently pass before my eyes; yet these plains are all wretched and useless. Without habitations, without water, without trees, without mountains. Why then, and the case is not particular to myself, have these arid wastes taken so firm a hold on my memory? Why have not the still more level, the greener and more fertile Pampas, which are serviceable to mankind, produced an equal impression? I can scarcely analyze these feelings, but it must be partly owing to the free scope to the mind. The plains of Patagonia are boundless for they are scarcely passable, and hence unknown. They bear the stamp of having lasted for ages, and there appears no limit to their duration through future time. If, as the ancients supposed, the flat earth was surrounded by an impassable breadth of water, or by deserts heated to an intolerable excess, who would not look to these last boundaries to man's knowledge with deep but ill-defined sensations?*

Linear time, upon which Darwin drew the marvel of evolution, had apparently gone missing for him in the Patagonia wastelands. They didn't shatter his psyche like a hurled vase. And they didn't, from the sound of it, dissolve his self. But the "ill-defined sensations" stuck with him for all his days. They also underscored how conditioned we are by natural cycles, how our sense of reality derives largely from predictable intervals. Stretch those over "The End of the Earth" and our perspectives come unmoored. As New York drama critic and nature writer, Joseph Krutch, noted in *A Study and a Confession* (1929), "Of the thought of something without beginning and presumably without end, of something which is . . . organized without any end in view, the mind reels."

From Charles Darwin to modern writers like David George Haskell, across all time and place, nature writing made clear that if we jump too deeply into the Big Empty, our minds will likely reel. It can also fly apart. It was reassuring to confirm how others had found the tragic key in the silent, empty reaches, yet for all of this, nothing much felt resolved. It still felt like I was jogging in the dark, clawing up a mountain with no summit. I put aside nature writing and plodded on.

It took an age to confirm my intuition, that the poison was the medicine. Strangely, the resolution came not through discovering another state to zero out the first one. Rather, the trick was to stop resisting the yawning emptiness that had tracked me down on The Watchtower, which I'd reeled from and fought off as if my life depended on it, and which fried my circuits in the bargain. Even when I'd dug my heels into the Big Empty, I was basically demanding nature to confirm that what I'd experienced, and what scores of nature writers had labored to put into words, was somehow mistaken. The void was full of rainbows. And Santa's bag is full.

At some level before words I'd clung to those childhood beliefs, and the feelings attached, till they melted in my hands. Every effort I made to try to explain or reason through this process, even to myself, felt preposterous. Zen parables were too fraught and inscrutable. Western attempts were no better. Had nobody found the words for this lightning?

Years later, and quite by chance, I found another long-forgotten piece by W. H. Hudson. Though the "heartless voids and immensities" initially shivered Hudson's timbers, his fear was time-bound, as was mine. We never pine over the eons before we were born, when we didn't exist. Who cares? Yet a future without us is a tragic and ghastly thought. Stranger still is that a clock never ticks in the Castle, where *before* and *after* are empty terms. As a thought or concept this counts for nothing. But our fear is real as fire when dark, empty silence swallows us alive. What lies behind that fear? If a person answers no other question, they should attempt to answer that one. W. H. Hudson meant to find out when he saddled up his horse and rode back into the Patagonia wasteland.

"Not once, nor twice, nor thrice," Hudson wrote in *Idle Days in Patagonia* (1893), "but day after day I returned to this solitude, going to it in the morning as if to attend a festival, and leaving it only when hunger and thirst and the westering sun compelled me."

One day he fell into a "novel state of mind."

I had become impossible of reflection; the mind had suddenly transformed itself from a thinking machine into a machine for some other unknown purpose. To think was like setting into motion a noisy engine in my brain; and there was something there that made me be still, and I was forced to obey. My state was one of suspense and watchfulness; yet I had no expectation of meeting with an adventure, and felt as free from apprehension as I feel now sitting in a room in London. The change in me was just as great and wonderful as if I had changed my identity from that of another man or animal; but at the time I was powerless to wonder at or speculate about it; the state seemed familiar rather than strange; and although accompanied by a strong feeling of elation, I did not know it—did not know that something had come between me and my intellect—until I lost it and returned to my former self—to thinking and the old insipid existence.

This wasn't bros in the backcountry. This wasn't about then and now, male or female, causes and effects, identities, beliefs, none of that. These are merely artifact. Silt. Once it settles, what remains? Hudson later added:

> *If there is such a thing as historical memory in us, is it not strange that the sweetest moment in any life pleasant or dreary, should be when nature draws near to it, and, taking up its neglected instrument, plays a fragment of some ancient melody, long unheard of on the earth . . . restoring instantaneously the old vanquished harmony between organism and environment.*

Out in the Patagonia wastelands, the boundary between Hudson and the frightening world "out there," steeped in thoughts, issues, importance, religion, paradigms, and equations—all these things simply dissolved. And so did his fear. He touched the Holy Grail, known and recognized only later, when he once more returned to his former self and his "right mind." If Hudson can serve as guide for our own experiences, it's crucial to realize what he didn't say, which is commonly decreed in twenty-first-century nature writing, a fact not lost on David Haskell in *The Forest Unseen* (2012):

> *The many stories of the universe from which we sprang provides transcendent power, inscrutable complexity, and humbling vastness. When we get a taste of these we're inclined to preach the revelation to others.*

Hudson could only chuckle at this for one reason: The Big Empty, the Castle—however you choose to put it—is entirely lacking in qualities. Nothing is there. No perspective or self-reflection, no location, no size, no measurements, no stuff, no concepts, including notions of the void.

Anyone returning from the wilderness as if fallen from a star, all shiny and strange and full of revelations, has at best merely peered into the Castle, a peeping Tom who didn't drop and let Nature make them over in Her own image. The adventure is not some philosophy that can be sought. Once swallowed, the old vanquished harmony simply occurs.

Perhaps the adventure was best summed up by my friend Bilbo, the former stick-up artist who now leads youth offenders culled from halfway houses and detox centers into the dark silence of Kentucky caverns, which "somehow, drains out the bad. Drop at a time. But I really don't know how it all works. Only that it does—for some."

The "some" who are not initially frightened off are made of different stuff than me, or of the bulk of nature writers quoted in this essay. They certainly are not the mystical pirates who have pilfered phrases like primordial nothingness and fluffed them into caricatures—codified, purified, demystified, and branded as the ambrosia of vision quests and walkabouts. Those who pushed through their fear don't present themselves as exalted anthologies. They lingered in the eye of the tornado, and experienced the living daylights.

But so what? How is any of this relevant to everyday life—not in caves, deserts, and remote rock ledges, but where the rubber meets the road where we live? It harks, I believe, back to the streams of knowing and being mentioned by Coleridge.

We can know certain things through objective data. Another type of knowing can only be had through immersive experience. We might read a treatise about apples, for example, with all the facts and figures, but the moment we bite into the apple we come to know what the data can never disclose. The beauty of Nature is found in Her things, but the power is condensed in Her silence, stillness, and monotone spaces, where the "old vanquished harmony between organism and environment" is finally restored through the resolution of opposites. Nature writing is art. A depiction. But the best of it is holy writing because the old harmony sounds between the lines, lines all the more treasured because they are written in rain.

Only through experiencing my own impermanence at terrifying depth would I ever have treasured the miracle of particles jumping from the void and forming up into rivers, trees, and people who, somehow, could come to love me, and the bittersweet fact that none of it lasts. Only when the Big Empty had drained me of pride, fear, and specialness could I begin to grasp the specialness of everyone and everything in creation, and to realize that violence, injustice, and indifference toward the planet and to others is a form of suicide.

A few weeks ago I found a magazine left on a plane and read an article about the Japanese art of *kintsugi* ("golden joinery," or "golden repair"), where broken pottery is pieced back together by way of soldered gold, silver, or platinum seams. "When a bowl, teapot or precious vase falls and breaks into a thousand pieces, we throw them away angrily and regretfully. Yet there is an alternative that highlights and enhances the breaks thus adding value to the broken object."

We're all partial and unfinished. We're all shattered. If Nature is good for nothing else, it's to rearrange, for a minute or a week, the chaotic fragments of our lives into a harmonious whole more striking that the original, the scars standing out like gold and silver solder. It never lasts but the experience of wholeness lingers, like perfume on a pillow, and every moment is found money. This is the promise of The Remote.

I AM IN THAT I AM.

Epilogue:
For All Mankind

We were three days up a river in the wilds of Brazil. The surrounding jungle was razed for 5 square miles, the fringe a splintered dam of logs crackling with flames and hissing in the downpour. Raw sewage clashed with the ripe smell of worked earth as we approached a seething hive of ex-cons, ex-barbers, ex-doctors, even ex-priests, swimming in mud. The racket swelled and the smoke thickened as we trudged to the brink of the massive open pit mine and peered inside.

Two hundred feet below were 40,000 itinerant prospectors—*garimpeiros*—nearly naked, glazed in sweat and muck and rain, a thunderous livid mud hole of flashing shovels and writhing backs attacking a sloppy grid of claims averaging 20 feet square. A dozen men, hip to hip and ass to ass, worked each tiered plot. I saw men slither into holes while others were dragged out by their ankles, bags of dirt clutched in their hands as all around men shoveled and swung axes and mauls and levered huge stones with pry bars. I watched a man turn to piss and get a pickax through his foot, and the men fought and the one opened up the other's forehead to the bone as a dozen others piled on but the surrounding throng hardly noticed and never stopped.

A train of maybe 5,000 men trudged through the mud in an endless loop, humping enormous bags of soppy dirt up a steep slope, legs shin deep and churning, finally stumbling to the summit of a mountain of tailings and dropping their bags and collapsing as if dead except for their heaving ribs. Others, also by the thousands, as if standing on each other's shoulders, hunched under the huge wet sacks, teetered up a web of creaky bamboo ladders, some 50 feet high, linked via crumbling terraces.

Up top we watched the bags dumped and sluiced and panned by 10,000 other men while the carriers, sheathed in muck, rose wearily and joined the loop for another load from the wallowing sump, every task done by hand, the toil and wretchedness heightened by taskmasters screaming at the workers, who had little chance of getting rich and less chance of getting paid—40,000 muddy men, effectively slaves, sustained by jungle tubers and coconut juice and the handful of millionaires strutting around the mud.

One of them, featured in *Época*, a popular Brazilian daily, was Guilhermino Caixeta, the twenty-three-year-old son of subsistence farmers from Cuiaba. He'd dug out a nugget big as an attaché case and had bought a rancho in Borba with 12,000 head of cattle. He even gave his folks a job. As peons. I figured Guilhermino was still down in the mud owing to a virus known as *febre do ouro*, gold fever in English, a demonic soul sickness where otherwise healthy people stream in from the four corners hoping to catch it.

Out beyond the swamp and the blazing shoal of trees I shuttered a photo of a spoonbill perched in a solitary jacaranda tree, peering down at a wilderness that no conscience, no soul, no God could endure. Only the *garimpeiros* could. Somewhere down there was their redemption. Somewhere down there was gold.

We forded back to the barge, climbed aboard, and forged on, the pilot's face pouring sweat and fixed upriver, like a man stalked from behind. Everything here was stalked from behind, from downriver.

Two days above the mine we passed the last boat scouring the riverbed for gold. Another day and we were past the last miner and the final logging camp and into primary terrain. The forest reared higher, the river narrowed, the current quickened, the boat slowed.

We hugged the bank against the current and plied through curtains of green light slanting down from the trees. The native Caboclos called it *la salon verde*, the green room. Gnarled ropes looped down, dangling in midair, flecked with black orchids and strangler figs. Bullfrogs croaked from fetid streams emptying into the river, and twice we passed coves of mangroves and the mad chorus of howler monkeys.

The forest grew close and immense and the slender aisles between trees darkened. Late that afternoon the sky caught fire between rags of clouds, and the river, flat and still, shined like liquid gold. An Indian paddled by, a huge manatee in the floor of his dugout. The Indian's chin was smeared red with annatto and on both sides of his face a tattooed streak ran from the corner of his mouth to his temple. He neither ignored nor acknowledged us, just slowly rode the current downstream, the tail of the huge mammal twitching and flashing in the light. We walked along the barge all the way to the stern, and we kept watching the Indian till far in the distance he fused with the flaming water.

This was twenty-five years ago, and we couldn't have imagined that the creeping juggernaut downstream could have ever made it this far. Last year, it did, and *la salon verde*, a hallowed domain if ever there was one, was lost forever.

The wanton destruction of our wilderness areas is usually fueled by some strain of *febre de ouro*. It just looks different than the Brazilian article, and the rhetoric is more deceptive. The claim that strip-mining the mountainside "creates jobs" justifies plundering wilderness areas and nature preserves so long as those authoring the destruction throw a few dollars at the workers. So we go for the short dollar by destroying nonrenewable resources, an unsustainable practice often countered by the lie that technology can reverse any collateral damage. Our insanity is to stand by and let shortsighted people orchestrate our extinction, believing that the future will take care of itself. This might have been so before the eighteenth century and the Industrial Revolution, but it's no longer the case—of this we may be sure.

Regaining our sanity in the hopes of surviving requires revisiting the age-old premise of *inherent* value. For decades the worth and usefulness of everything from old-growth forests to freshwater lakes hinged on our ability to monetize the "commodity" found there. It falls on everyone to revise this thinking and to clear the decks of those who can't. Shaming, blaming, and ranting are opening and perhaps essential steps in raising awareness, but such strategies more likely breed resistance than understanding and change. There's little time to resolve our differences, and demanding amends, on moral grounds, is not an action plan. As happens in critical conflicts, "the wounded must lead," or we're done for. Only a unified front can negotiate a way out of the mess we've created. Somewhere between picking up trash on the trail and addressing Congress lies a task for us all in securing our planet's survival—even for those seeking to destroy it.